The Green Guide
for Business

The Green Guide for Business

Chris Goodall

with contributions from
Craig Simmons of **Best Foot Forward**

First published in Great Britain in 2009 by
*Green*Profile
Profile Books Ltd
3a Exmouth House
Pine Street
London EC1R 0JH
www.profilebooks.com

A CIP catalogue record for this book is available from the British Library.

ISBN 978 1 84668 874 4 (Profile edition)
ISBN 978 1 84668 878 2 (Barclays edition)

Designed and typeset in Minion by Sue Lamble
sue@lambledesign.demon.co.uk
Indexing by Indexing Specialists (UK) Ltd
Printed and bound in Britain by CPI Bookmarque, Croydon, Surrey

This book was originally produced for Barclays Commercial Bank customers.

Contents

Foreword
by Marcus Agius

The global economy is facing its most difficult time for decades. In the current economic climate, business leaders will naturally be concerned with short-term, business-critical decisions, and there are many who will say that we should put off action on climate change and focus on more immediate challenges.

I disagree. Addressing green issues is not incompatible with commercial decision-making, regardless of whether the economy is growing or facing recession.

Being a green business is part of being an economically sustainable business. Green businesses, both large and small, have lean processes and use resources efficiently. They have committed employees who value working for a responsible business. They scan the horizon for signs of changes in consumer behaviour and in government policy. They innovate and are among the first movers into new environmental markets. They are resilient to the changes that the low-carbon economy will inevitably bring.

These factors are increasingly relevant to business leaders as sustainability becomes part of 'business as usual' strategic management.

Two years ago, when I was asked by Richard Lambert, the Director-General of the Confederation of British Industry, if I would serve on a board he was proposing to establish to determine the response of British industry to the climate change crisis, I needed little encouragement to do so. Nor did eighteen other business leaders including representatives from Shell, Siemens, Tesco and Rolls-Royce. In fact, Richard's invitation was refused by no one.

I was not surprised. Climate change is a risk to sustainable business shared by everyone; it is the challenge of our generation. Customers around the world are looking to governments and business for leadership on climate change. They are tough critics, persuaded by decisive action, and not by words.

Being an economically sustainable business brings huge challenges, but there are also opportunities. I have seen many highly successful businesses finding a niche for themselves in new markets, from energy efficiency to rethinking traditional building materials.

They are amongst many organisations which have invested heavily in green products or initiatives. They are frequently more efficient and cost effective than carbon-intensive alternatives. As such, their value actually becomes greater in time of economic hardship. Indeed, the clean technology industry as a whole has continued to shrug off the economic downturn in recent months, and figures for 2008 estimate that total investment will rise to $150bn, up 60 per cent from 2007. Your challenge is to find those opportunities for your business, and it is a personal challenge.

For me, I want to be able to look back when the global economy recovers and say that Barclays upheld its commitment to the environment. Not because of a philanthropic belief, but because in the long-term it is in the best interests of our customers and so of our shareholders also. Our objective is to make sustainability not just something we do for an hour each Thursday when times are good. It needs to be an intrinsic part of our day-to-day practices so that it becomes business as usual, come rain or shine.

This book is a guide for businesses of all sizes who want to reap the benefits of being more environmentally sustainable. It is full of practical advice to help you to focus on the issues that are most important to your business, and to begin making positive – and smart – changes.

Marcus Agius
Chairman, Barclays

Introduction

When economic times are tough, why would anybody bother to try to build a greener business? Won't a deteriorating business climate mean that green issues will cease to be a principal concern?

No. A green business will cope better with adversity. It will be more resilient and leaner than an equivalent business that is built on excess use of energy, over-consumption of scarce resources and a lax attitude to waste. A green business that performs as a responsible global citizen will have a better relationship with its customers, employees, suppliers and investors.

Here are some surprising observations from later in this book to back up this claim:

- If you let employees control the light levels in their offices, they will generally set them at a lower level than a professional lighting engineer. What's more, they will generally work with more accuracy. So you save money, reduce carbon emissions and create a more efficient environment. Give them some access to natural light as well, and productivity will rise even further.

- Send your young employees on an eco-driving course, and their petrol consumption will fall sharply. They will drive better. And will also have far fewer accidents, meaning that you save money on staff absences, insurance and car-repair bills.

● Farmers keep potatoes in moist storage conditions to stop the crop from drying out and losing valuable weight. But if you make crisps, you prefer drier potatoes as it takes less energy to fry them. Walkers Crisps now pays its producers not to keep the potatoes in damp conditions; the farmer gains because storage is easier and Walkers benefits from lower energy costs.

● Video-conferencing does more than just help reduce corporate bills for air travel for senior executives. By allowing junior employees to 'meet' their colleagues at similar levels across the world via video-conferencing, a sense of cooperation is immediately fostered and it becomes easier for everyone to work together more productively.

● Properly looked after, PCs with low power consumption should last much longer that their more wasteful equivalents. Energy efficiency means lower electricity bills, but it is equally prudent that you only replace your machines every five years.

Becoming green isn't just some joyless exercise to take a few per cent off your energy bill – it is a positive move both because it helps a business work through the tough times and, properly directed, it also helps improve the longer-term prospects for your organisation.

This book examines the ways in which the thoughtful business-person can think about making their organisation leaner and less wasteful. It offers a large number of practical tips but also looks at how building a green organisation is good for productivity and morale. Look at any list of the most respected companies in the UK and it is no accident that almost all of them have effective environmental policies. Innovative and exciting organisations all seem to be taking climate change issues seriously. This is no coincidence – good companies are green.

A resilient company now has t
be green. There is certainly ne
conflict between profits and th
environment.

Be ambitious

A green business will be more
profitable and resilient

Before we get into the detail of *how* to go green, let's take a quick look at the business case for taking such a path. That means touching on the typical costs and benefits, the uncertainties surrounding climate change and resource depletion, and the different levels of environmental commitment that a business or organisation can show.

Why go green?

Creating a green company is simply the right thing to do. As well as being good for your business, reducing waste and energy use is good for the planet – and for the future. But how will becoming green help your business weather difficult times? In short, making your company more focused on environmental objectives will have five principal benefits. It will help you to:

- Reduce costs
- Build staff loyalty and improve recruitment
- Secure loyalty from customers who increasingly require suppliers to show green credentials
- Understand supply chains and the way your products are used. This reduces vulnerability to resource shortages, changes in regulation and to variations in buyer behaviour.

● Take advantage of new product development and new market opportunities.

Let's take a look at these points.

Reducing costs: energy and beyond

Adding a thin green veneer to your business will add to your expenses. A wind turbine on the roof or a decision to provide compostable plastic bags for your customers will not make a substantial difference to your environmental credentials. It may also be expensive. But really getting to grips with the amount of energy and materials you use will offer appreciable financial return. This is true both for major users of fossil fuels, like airlines, and for small companies working from a rented suite in a large office building.

However, we should be clear that the direct costs of gas and electricity don't matter much to most organisations. Yes, easyJet and Ryanair's financial results are affected dramatically by oil prices but service companies generally have utility bills that are a small portion of total costs, representing perhaps 1 or 2 per cent of the organisation's overall expenses. Many businesses are barely conscious of the bills they get from their utility company even after price rises, and few have mounted a determined effort to moderate their energy consumption. For example, the primary school I pass on the way to work leaves its boilers and refrigerators working as usual over the school holidays; the computer-aided design company I then cycle past still uses old-fashioned light bulbs.

If power costs are such a small fraction of the budget of a typical organisation, is it worth actually working to reduce your energy consumption? You probably need to look at the issue slightly differently. It isn't just your own electricity bills you are paying – you should also remember that everything you buy contains 'embodied' energy, often in large amounts. A pack of copier paper contains five kilowatt hours of energy used in manufacturing and another couple of kilowatt hours to package it and bring it to your door. The energy content of just two of these reams would run all the appliances and the lighting in the typical UK home for over a day. Similarly, a new executive car equates to several more tonnes of carbon dioxide in the global atmosphere, mostly from the manufacture of the metals used in the vehicle. You may not realise it, but you are paying for the energy use of your suppliers.

Essentially, the energy bills you receive represent the tip of a very large iceberg. The last time the figure was properly calculated in 2005, energy represented about 5 per cent of the modern economy. Since then, price rises will have pushed this up. Now, perhaps 8–10 per cent of the cost of the inputs of an organisation – direct and embodied – will be for energy. It clearly makes sense to use less fuel and power but also to choose your suppliers on the basis of how seriously *they* take energy efficiency. We all know that the prices of gas, electricity and motor fuels can vary unpredictably. However, careful reductions of energy use will always save you money.

And it is not just energy. A business focusing on green issues also needs to find ways of reducing the use of raw materials and outside supplies. An environmentally aware business doesn't simply look to cut the use of materials as a way of saving embodied energy costs, but also as a means of reducing the amount of the world's resources employed to produce its products. One obvious example is packaging. Cardboard is a cheap and effective way of protecting goods in transit, but most suppliers use virgin materials. In an era of plenty, this seemed a sensible approach, as it is usually cheaper than buying recycled board. The same is true of plastics made from petrochemicals. But it is not going to stay that way – at some time in the future, recycled packaging materials are going to become cheaper than their virgin equivalents. A well-managed organisation should be examining now how to develop a supply chain that minimises the use of external materials, particularly those newly made from limited resources.

Ask yourself a simple question: which way are all the trends pointing? Oil prices may go up and down, but in ten or twenty years' time do you think that fossil fuel prices will be higher or lower than today? Many of tomorrow's large capital projects will still be operating then. If you think green issues are going to become more and more important, investment decisions today must be biased in favour of those options that use the least energy and are most economical in the use of resources.

Building staff loyalty and improving recruitment

Some people don't particularly care about environmental issues – they go to work to earn a living, not to save the world. It would be foolish to pretend otherwise. But inside your organisation will be a small percentage of staff who really are concerned about the company's attitude to the environment. They genuinely don't want to work for an employer that is indifferent or antagonistic to green issues. Although staff with strong principles can sometimes seem a mixed blessing, these people will often embody the core values that organisations seek to project to the outside world. You need them. Without these individuals your company would find it much more difficult to understand the increasing number of customers with green demands or to forecast how environmental concerns will change the business environment.

Imagine you run a soft-drinks manufacturing firm. You know that your industry has potential image problems: your products are linked to obesity, they are sometimes blamed for hyperactivity in children and you are the target of activists in developing countries who are concerned about the impact of your bottling plants on the depletion of local water supplies. The long-term prosperity of your business completely depends on remoulding it so that it meets the demands of external stakeholders. The green idealists in your business are your best link to the world outside, helping to understand and interpret the strong messages you get from activists and customers. You need to keep them, but you won't be able to unless you improve the company's underlying commitment to green behaviour, not only as expressed in your products but also in the way you run your business. This is not always a pain-free process; the green idealists may want you to make changes that are expensive and inconvenient. But without these people you will inevitably always be late in reacting to the environmental pressures put on the organisation.

For potential new recruits, the issue is often more important still. An organisation's attitude to green issues is often a key part of the appeal to its best employees. Sir Michael Rake, the chairman of BT, said recently that his organisation faced twin challenges: dealing with climate change and winning 'the war for talent' – getting the top-quality individuals to come and work for the company. These two issues are closely related. A business or public sector body that takes the climate change issue seriously is likely to be particularly attractive to some of the best potential recruits. To work for an organisation that is seen as a leader on green issues adds to the perceived status of being an employee. And, unsurprisingly, for an organisation that faces potential problems of public image – a defence hardware company or a fast-food firm, for example – a poor rating on green issues will be enough to steer many individuals away from applying to the firm. Human resources managers should be actively campaigning for green commitments in order to make recruitment of the best candidates easier.

Securing customer loyalty

Customers increasingly demand that their suppliers show a verifiable commitment to green behaviour. This isn't just about ephemeral changes to packaging or vague promises to plant some trees in a forest far away. Sophisticated buyers, whether individuals buying clothes in Marks & Spencer or government agencies deciding on £100 million contracts, demand that the goods and services they buy embody wider green attributes. An increasing portion of people buying groceries want ethically sourced, low-carbon, minimally packaged food. At the other end of the spectrum, government bodies often say that large suppliers must have ISO 14001 certification (a check on an organisation's approach to environmental issues). Or they demand that suppliers have signed up to programmes that demand transparency of accounting for carbon emissions, such as the Carbon Disclosure Project (CDP). For example, Wal-Mart, the world's largest grocery retailer, and owner of Asda in the UK, will soon require that all its business partners provide details of greenhouse-gas emissions to the CDP. You won't get business from an increasingly large number of organisations unless you show demonstrable commitment to lower carbon emissions in the way that you do business.

Customers, small and large, want your organisation to be trying to manage its emissions downwards and reduce its use of materials. They are partly trying to ensure that they get good value from you, but they are also aware of the potential damage to their brand if your company is seen to be a poor environmental performer. Imagine that you are trying to build a public image that stresses your green credentials as a food producer. You want your product to be the number-one choice for the increasing number of ethical consumers. A newspaper finds out that your main supplier is indirectly getting its agricultural raw materials from recently deforested areas on the edge of the Amazon. Rightly or wrongly, it is accused of causing loss of forest. The impact on your business is immediate: you should have checked all the way back up the supply chain. The damage to your brand image will take years to remedy.

It's true that many business and government bodies are not really interested in sustainability issues and their apparent concern for ethical sourcing is more imaginary than real. Nevertheless, the demands that they place on you, their supplier, are genuine: even the most cynical company works to protect the value of its brand from erosion arising from embarrassing disclosures of poor practices in suppliers. This may seem a remote possibility, but it is not. As an example, a fast-food supplier was recently forced into a humiliating climbdown after its containers were found to be made in a factory emitting large quantities of an extremely potent gas linked to global warming.

Understanding supply chains to reduce vulnerability to shocks

Some of the luxury German car manufacturers have been fighting against the imposition of tighter emissions rules imposed by the EU. Many of their models are gas-guzzlers, and the companies will need to make wrenching changes to meet the proposed fuel economy rules. Other motor manufacturers such as Citroën, which builds some of the lowest-emission cars on the road, face a much less stressful challenge. Its business is far less vulnerable to changes in government regulation. Some manufacturers don't appear to have seen the threat of mandatory emissions caps coming; as a result, their shareholders will suffer. Make no mistake, environmental regulation is going to get tougher and tougher. If your business doesn't accurately predict the speed and intensity of new green laws, it will be at a competitive disadvantage.

It's not just regulation. Your customers don't want to buy products that use a lot of energy in their operation. These days, who wants a car with high fuel consumption, or a fridge that uses twice as much electricity as the best product on the market or a piece of clothing that needs to be washed at 60 degrees when alternatives only require 30 degrees? Your business is threatened not just if you use too much expensive energy but also if consumers face high fuel costs to use your product. At the moment, you may think that your customers, both business and consumer, don't really care. And you may be right. But, for example, a fridge, a television, a domestic boiler or a car will now cost more to run over the course of its life than it costs to buy. It can't be long before apparently indifferent consumers start seeking out the products that offer sustained economy in use. Most business customers reached this stage some time ago.

You are also at the mercy of your suppliers' inefficiency. For example, perhaps you chose a supplier of platinum catalysts that offered you the least expensive deal at the time. They were cheapest because they didn't bother to capture and recycle the surplus metal left at the end of the production process. Between 2004 and mid-2008, the price of the metal quadrupled. Now it is the company that had worked out how to recycle the waste platinum that offers the best prices, but it no longer has the capacity to supply your needs. Because you didn't understand the wastefulness of your supplier, you have made yourself vulnerable to unpredictable price changes and sudden shortages.

In the USA, and also increasingly in the UK, data centres cannot get the extra electricity they need to expand their businesses. Their supply is capped because of local shortages of power in places like California and the Thames Valley. Some companies in the USA have got round this problem by supplying their own renewable energy. As one example, some of Google's new data centres are powered by solar energy and its growth is not curtailed by its reliance on the increasingly fragile public supplies of electricity. A green business is often a more resilient one, less vulnerable to prices shocks and shortages of materials.

You may feel that none of these issues really applies to you and your business. Perhaps you work in a small office alongside a few other professionals. Your electricity bill is moderate and you do the basic housekeeping, such as recycling your paper and soft-drink cans. It might seem that you don't have much to gain from a difficult switch to becoming a much greener business.

I know an architects' practice just like this. They thought they were immune from threat. They weren't wasteful, they just had never really thought about the issues. Then one day they went to pitch for an important piece of work for one of the UK's best-known companies. It was a big project that would have looked superb on their list of achievements for decades to come. They walked into the presentation confident in their proposed designs. There in attendance was the CEO of the company, an individual known to take sustainability issues seriously and someone who speaks regularly on the topic. He wasn't really interested in the appearance of the building they proposed, instead launching into questions about expected electricity consumption, the amount of concrete required and the use of recycled building materials. The architects failed to secure the job. Not only did they not know the answers about the new building, they couldn't speak from experience else-where on other projects. They couldn't even boast about what they had done in their own office. To add to the embarrass-ment, the CEO gave them some useful tips on the way out of the room about how to cut electricity use in air-conditioned buildings.

Another example is a university that I know. Its halls of resi-dence are some of the most wasteful buildings I have seen.

Decades of poor maintenance, combined with lack of interest in energy efficiency in new buildings, have resulted in increasing utility use. Energy prices are shooting up, throwing budgets into disarray and forcing the institution to prune some of its academic activities.

Some institutions come face to face with difficult issues when they decide to go green and simply back away from taking action. Last year, I did a carbon audit for an extremely successful church. Its pews are full several times a week and it takes its social responsibilities very seriously. It wanted to cut carbon emissions substantially to demonstrate its commitment to looking after the Creator's planet. It thought that by buying its electricity from a green supplier it would prompt a real improvement. Actually, by far the largest proportion of the church's emissions was the congregation's annual ski trip to the Alps, dwarfing all the other sources of emissions. Tactfully, I tried to point this out and was politely shown the door. Clearly, saving the planet is going to involve some difficult decisions for organisations trying to act ethically.

No organisation is immune from the changes that climate change and high energy prices are bringing about. Every organisation is going to have to move beyond green windowdressing to substantial changes in the way it does business. This book provides a framework for thinking about how best to build sustainability in your office, factory, school, hospital or community centre.

As a business-person or manager in the not-for-profit sector, what do you really need to know about climate change and the other green issues of today? In the swirling currents of arguments and debate, how do you work out what is important and what is not?

The debate on climate change

It has been known for over a hundred years that the carbon dioxide (CO_2) in the atmosphere helps keep the planet warm. Along with water vapour, methane and other global warming gases, CO_2 traps heat and makes the earth habitable. Temperatures are about 33 degrees Celsius higher than they otherwise would be without these gases.

Burning fossil fuels adds more and more CO_2 to the atmosphere, and concentrations are rising. All other things being equal, there is extremely strong reason to believe that increased carbon dioxide means higher temperatures. Although carbon dioxide forms only a tiny part of the atmosphere – a fraction of one part in a thousand – almost all scientific calculations suggest that man's actions are likely to add to the world's average surface temperatures. The likelihood is that today's global temperatures are over 0.7 degrees Celsius warmer than they would have been without the extra CO_2 we have added to the atmosphere. And even if carbon dioxide concentrations stabilised tomorrow, the temperature will keep on going up for many decades.

Temperatures aren't rising in a predictable or steady way. In fact, the hottest year on record was 1998, ten years ago, although several more recent years have almost matched the level. But taken as a whole, the first eight years of the 21st century appear to have seen global temperatures higher than any equivalent period in recent history. Of course, people debate the reasons for the erratic but increasingly obvious temperature increase and argue about whether it will continue in the future. The global atmosphere is such a complex and poorly understood system that we can never really be certain about causes and effects. Nevertheless, all of the respected individuals called on to assess whether we should act to mitigate the threat from climate change have told us that the penalty from inaction is far greater than the financial costs of beginning the slow process of reducing greenhouse-gas emissions. As a result of the unanimity of the verdicts, the government inserted into the Climate Change Bill a legal obligation on the UK to cut its emissions by 80 per cent by 2050.

We need to acknowledge some of the huge uncertainties:

- How much impact on temperatures does CO_2 have? Do we understand the precise link between carbon dioxide concentrations and global average temperature levels? The honest answer to this is probably 'no' and much more work is needed to understand just how sensitive the world's climate is to increasing stocks of greenhouse gases in the atmosphere.

- Will temperature increases accelerate once we get beyond a certain point? Above a 2-degree increase above pre-industrial levels, how likely is it that we will see irreversible future rises? What is the chance of rapid rises of 10 degrees Celsius or more, something that occurred in instances of rapid global warming long ago? Talk privately to a level-headed climate scientist and he or she will be likely to say that very large rises in temperature, well beyond the figures published in the press, are possible. The likelihood may be 1 per cent or it may be 20 per cent, but the risks of total catastrophe are uncomfortably large.

- How will temperature change affect sea levels? Crucially, how fast will the ice caps of Greenland and Antarctica melt? Although sea-level rises are clearly getting more rapid, there is considerable uncertainty as to likely level of change in fifty or a hundred years. It might be 50 cm or it might be 3 metres; the world can probably cope with the former, but the latter would leave many large cities and swathes of the most productive croplands under water.

- Will the changes to the world's rainfall and the rate of glacier melt seriously affect the availability of water for people and for crops? The rapid rate of melting of Himalayan and other mountain ice may mean that the world's main rivers eventually have no water supply to feed them during summer. Billions of people rely on these sources of drinking water.

- Just how dangerous are temperature rises to the amount of food production around the world? Fifteen years ago, many people thought that global warming might actually add to the productivity of farmlands and forests. Now, the evidence is that many important food-producing areas, such as southern China, will see falling yields. This is potentially catastrophic for living standards.

To an extent perhaps unappreciated by many of the world's politicians and policy-makers, there is much that we don't understand yet about the consequences of our experiment with the global atmosphere. We can expect that the scientific debate will run for a long time yet. As the distinguished Oxford economist Paul Klemperer put it recently:

The continuing scientific uncertainty about the pace of climate change should make us more concerned, not less. And it is those who doubt the climatologists' models who should be the most frightened.

Look at the various reports of the UN's Intergovernmental Panel on Climate Change (IPCC) and Klemperer's point is reinforced. As the scientists have done more work, the range of potential futures for our climate has widened. Despite the huge effort put into climate change research, we appear to know little more – and perhaps even less – now than we thought we did ten years ago. But the lack of 100 per cent certainty isn't an excuse for inaction. Business-people know that they have to deal with probability and chance in everything that they do. Do we stop the launch of a new product just because there is a risk of failure? Or halt all research and development programmes because they might not succeed? Similarly, we all insure our buildings against fire, although we know there is only a tiny probability of a loss in any particular year.

Running a successful organisation, public or private, requires managers to continuously scan the horizon for risks and opportunities. Which company waits until it is 100 per cent certain that a competitor's new technology will make its own product superfluous? Which manager ignores a known health and safety risk to employees, even if the chances of injury are quite small? Or who creates long-term plans on the basis that economic growth will continue at a relentlessly stable 2.5 per cent per year? Good managers know that actions need to be taken even when information is inadequate and the degree of risk is uncertain. It is the same with global warming and the associated problem of volatile energy prices and depletion of the world's mineral resources. No sensible person should ignore the risk of climate change, nor the opportunities it represents to create new markets and innovative ways of doing business.

Ben Verwaayen, the respected former CEO of BT, put this point in his own inimitably clear fashion when heading the CBI climate change taskforce:

Are we sure that climate change exists? I am sorry, but that is not a question for us. The best question for the business community is whether we can be certain that climate change presents a substantial risk; a risk that will have a profound impact on society and the economy. To this the answer is clearly 'yes'. And so, as with all substantial risks, it is vital to mitigate the danger.

Verwaayen is arguing that it is strongly in our interests to act as if global warming presents a substantial threat, even though this assumption may just possibly turn out to be wrong. But another question arises: why should individual companies or other organisations go through painful changes in order to use less energy or fewer other natural resources? If no single corporation, however large, can hope to make much of a difference to global emissions reductions, why should they bother? The answer is that even small companies are vulnerable to climate change; not necessarily in the sense that temperature and rainfall changes may directly affect their viability but because social and political trends will advantage those companies that have taken pre-emptive steps to green their operations.

Verwaayen's own former company, BT, provides a good example. Its telecommunications equipment is vulnerable to the increasing threat of major rain storms, and many of its assets are vulnerable to flooding. This makes precautionary measures sensible. But, in addition, BT uses over half of 1 per cent of UK electricity, meaning that it is threatened by any levy that raises the price of power, or any government policy that restricts its use. The company has reduced its exposure to risk by committing to get a large percentage of its future power needs from wind turbines on its own land. It is a world leader in reducing the electricity needs of its data centres and huge server farms. It has also used its strength as a large purchaser of energy to persuade its main suppliers to improve the power consumption of telecommunications equipment. This makes sense both to environmentalists and to the company's shareholders. Partly as a result of BT's unequivocal stance on the need to assume that climate change is happening and will require substantial changes at some stage in the future, investment funds that focus on sustainability are major purchasers of BT's stocks and bonds.

Many small companies don't face similar risks, and may not have shareholders with similar long-term horizons. For them, it may seem that there is little point in taking action. However in these cases, the threat from climate change is a different one. The issue they face is that companies like BT, one of the most important purchasers in the UK economy, will cease to buy from companies that aren't addressing the risks posed by climate change. Secondly, the most responsible, thoughtful employees will seek employment in institutions, like BT, with an attitude to climate change that is understood to be socially responsible and appropriately risk averse. Wasteful and irresponsible companies, however small, simply won't be able to attract the best people.

Of course, climate change could turn out to be more benign

than the current consensus suggests. It is conceivable that temperature rises could reverse and wind and rainfall patterns stabilise. No sensible company or public institution should deny this possibility. Perhaps, as some climate change sceptics say, the earth's cloud cover will increase as hotter temperatures cause more evaporation; increased cloudiness might halt temperature change. No careful business-person should run a company on the basis that the future is easily predictable. It may be as dangerous to listen to the most frightened of the world's scientists as it is to ignore them. The right approach is to try to maintain the most flexible organisation – one that can respond quickly to any environmental or policy changes. Betting the company on an inexorable, decades-long requirement to be increasingly green isn't as risky as turning your back on environmental issues, but it might cause its own problems.

Here's one example. Building your own renewable electricity generating capacity is probably a good idea – the likelihood is that fossil fuel-based energy is going to become more expensive as countries use regulation to nudge the economy more towards low-carbon sources. But there is a – usually unspoken – risk in doing this. You may be exposing your organisation to the risk of a sustained fall in electricity prices or technological obsolescence as new renewable technologies take over from ones we are accustomed to today. As previously stated, BT is investing heavily in wind energy and no one criticises it for this decision. But there are four or five alternative technologies that might well produce electricity at lower prices by 2020. By then, BT may have hundreds of millions of pounds of expensive assets, and the wind farms may then be a burden, not a competitive advantage. A headlong rush into green technology may not actually be the best corporate strategy. A careful and measured move almost certainly is.

Waste and resource depletion

Being green isn't just a matter of preparing for climate change. It is also working out how to use smaller amounts of the world's resources at the same time as growing a business and responding to customer needs. But the same issues apply. In all probability, the world has begun to exhaust some of its major mineral sources. And it is not just fossil fuels: the world supply of phosphate ores, a vital ingredient in most manufactured fertilisers, may also have peaked. And lithium may be in short supply when the world responds to the almost inevitable need to replace the internal combustion engine with electric cars. (The best current type of battery needs large amounts of this metal and supplies will almost certainly run short at some stage.)

The years 2007 and early 2008 saw unprecedented increases in the price of many of the world's crucial commodities, foodstuffs, minerals and metals. The more wasteful and careless the company, the worse was the impact of sharp escalations in the price of raw materials. It makes obvious sense to assume that we will see painful jumps in the price of many important resources, disrupting producers that are most profligate in their use.

Nevertheless, we can never be absolutely confident that the world is imminently running short of oil or of any of the ores of the world's major metals. So it would be wrong to run a business on the basis that plastics made from oil, or packaging material like steel cans, are inevitably going to get more expensive. Do not believe those who tell you that we can use simple rules to build a green business such as 'always minimise the use of packaging'. Actually, we need to make a more sophisticated analysis. Despite what some green consumer groups say, packaging is not always a bad thing. Goods are wrapped in plastic, cardboard, metal or paper partly for aesthetic reasons, but also because most products need protection from damage. Would it make sense to ship summer peaches from Italy without the use of thin plastic trays with shallow indentations to keep the fruit separate? It would not. The importer uses this protection for good reason, and it makes no sense to waste a third of the peaches in order to avoid all packaging. Each peach took energy and fertiliser to grow and transport, and the environmental waste of one fruit would be far greater than the fossil fuel used to make a 50 g plastic tray. Yes, it almost always makes sense to work out how to use design improvements to avoid needless expense, and there's no environmental reason to use plastic trays that are thicker than necessary. But that shouldn't mean that we need to get rid of all packaging.

A successful green business will be analytic in its assessment of how best to reduce its footprint. In chapter 2, we will look at the difficult issue of how to deal with customers and employees with misguided ideas about what is green and what is not. In general, it will usually make sense to design products that use the fewest and lightest components, and it should be possible to persuade suppliers and consumers that this is the case. In fact, if you don't know the carbon footprint of something you buy, the best way of guessing the number would be to weigh it – it's likely that the heavier it is, the more energy was used in its manufacture. The main exceptions to this rule are items made out of aluminium (which has a particularly high energy cost to make) and anything refined from large quantities of ore, such as gold. But otherwise you can usually say that something lighter is better than something heavier.

It is now usually beneficial to design for 100 per cent recyclability and many companies make this claim in their marketing literature. This will tend to reduce the total environmental impact of any product. But even more important is the need to design goods that will be recycled. Many products claim recyclability but are completely uneconomic to take apart and split into components. When buying something for your business, assess whether it can productively be recycled. Most cars and electronic goods can now be broken up usefully.

The other green issues

In addition to climate change and avoiding resource depletion, the third major plank when building a green business is 'social responsibility', or what I call good citizenship. Most large companies produce fat reports each year that detail how much they have done to protect the local environment or help disadvantaged groups. Some of these documents are extremely unconvincing, focusing on a few items of corporate windowdressing. Other companies do actually demonstrate a clear commitment to improving the world while at the same time making money for shareholders. Barclays, for example, has a worldwide programme for achieving 'carbon neutral' status as

23

well as diverse and inventive strategies for improving access to banking in the African countries in which it is such an important part of the financial system.

The reasons for the diversity in performance between the progressive companies and the laggards are all too clear. For much of the last 30 years, many people denied that businesses had any responsibility other than to make as much money in as short a period as possible. Though only rarely expressed as openly as this, most business-people had a deeply ingrained view that good citizenship should not be one of their business objectives – there was no place for what they saw as a sentimental belief in social responsibility. Those companies whose commitment to good corporate citizenship is lagging are still holding on to this intellectual current from the 1980s.

The progressive organisations have noticed that proper pursuit of corporate responsibility is a good way of building their business. Active involvement in community and social issues helps a company understand the environment in which it is trying to sell its products. It helps build the brand and gives employees a feeling that their employer is decent and responsible. The cost of good citizenship is usually not large and the returns are often substantial. The risks of not doing it are huge.

Five steps up the green ladder

We can all recognise the businesses that are merely making a token attempt to look green – one company promises to plant a tree every time you buy its product, another has placed a small wind turbine on its factory roof. To these businesses, becoming green is a matter of offering small gestures to improve the company's public image. These limited expenditures are probably a line in the marketing budget rather than being a central part of how the business wants to position itself for the long-term future. There's nothing wrong with these actions, but they are likely to have a tiny impact on the business's emissions. In fact, green gestures like this may actually damage a company's reputation if customers come to see them as pointless 'greenwash'.

Other companies recognise that a focus on environmental issues and social responsibility may become utterly central to the way a successful business operates. Some have already reinvented themselves. Vestas, the world-leading Danish wind turbine company, was making cranes and other industrial products when the first oil shock occurred in the early 1970s. It took a huge gamble and committed itself to the nascent wind turbine industry. After some unsuccessful experiments with unconventional designs, it settled on the three-bladed propeller that is now almost universal, and built a hugely successful and fast-growing global business.

Most companies lie somewhere on the spectrum between these two types of organisation. The ladder from greenwash to total commitment has the steps laid out in the diagram overleaf. Where does your organisation lie on this ladder? Where are your competitors? Would it make good business sense to move up another step? Most of this book examines useful examples of good housekeeping (step 1) and small capital expenditures, or 'quick wins' (step 2). Many businesses are, quite correctly, operating on these two steps in the ladder. But I also try to introduce as many illustrations as I can of projects higher up the ladder. It may be that ambitious

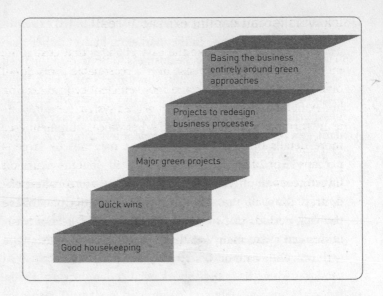

Basing the business entirely around green approaches

Projects to redesign business processes

Major green projects

Quick wins

Good housekeeping

schemes like these are inappropriate for your business at the moment. Nevertheless, good business planning demands that you scan the horizon for opportunities to use green thinking to make major changes in the way your organisation works.

Good housekeeping

The first step up is a small one. Companies can make real improvements with simple and often free housekeeping changes. Turning appliances off at night, adjusting office temperatures and switching to more efficient light bulbs can save considerable amounts of energy. Sensible changes to the company's policy on reimbursing motoring costs can encourage people to use trains and buses by ceasing to overpay for business car mileage.

Quick wins (small capital expenditures)

The next move is to make the easy changes that cost some money but repay the expense over a reasonable time. Small offices might install a new and more efficient central heating boiler, fit better lighting or put in place a system for automatically turning off computers and other office equipment (see more details on p. 106). The savings may not be large – perhaps 15 or 20 per cent of the energy bill – but the return on investment will often compare well with other capital expenditures. Most of the examples quoted in this book have payback periods of two years or less. The majority of businesses can make many relatively small changes of this type with very little pain or disruption.

Major green projects

Many organisations have begun to think about substantial green investments that would significantly change their carbon footprint. These tend to be costly, and will sometimes have unacceptable payback times. Examples include the installation of a combined heat and power boiler, the construction of a truly green headquarters building, in house anaerobic digestion of waste or a well-thought-through plan to reduce the electricity bill from running the corporate data centre. The payback time for these projects may be longer, but the long-term cost reductions may be significant.

Projects to redesign business processes

This is not just about saving money, but about rebuilding the way a business operates to benefit from a future world in which fossil fuel energy is extremely expensive or simply unavailable, or where climate change has become such a central issue that customers have significantly adjusted their buying behaviour. For example, Sierra Nevada Brewery, a rapidly growing beer producer in northern California, plans to make itself independent of grid electricity by installing fuel cells for heat and power and a large solar photovoltaic farm for electricity. Like several other US brewers, it is trying to make itself energy independent in order both to deal with the unreliability of local grid electricity and to improve its image in the eyes of customers. Walkers Crisps, the Pepsico subsidiary that makes a large fraction of the UK's salty snacks, seeks to buy all its potatoes from farms close to its Leicester factory. This reduces transport costs and allows the company to have closer business ties with its suppliers. Kingerlee Homes, a medium-sized construction company in Oxfordshire, invested large sums in developing the blueprint for eco-homes that both offered hugely improved energy efficiency and also met tough local planning requirements obliging builders to construct conventional stone-clad homes.

More generally, businesses can begin to introduce robust green procurement practices, begin the redesign of products to reflect climate change, and begin the process of incorporating a price of carbon dioxide into their own business plans. For example, BP has an internal trading system that obliges business units to pay for the carbon that they produce.

Basing the business entirely around green approaches

Not many companies have yet tried to wholly build their

business around a strategy that removes the need for fossil fuel energy, both in their own operations and those of their suppliers. Specialist renewable energy suppliers like Ecotricity, which constructs wind turbines on industrial sites, or Good Energy, the only 100 per cent renewable electricity supplier in the UK, are two examples. Jenny Hall runs a business in Lancashire that supplies boxes of organic vegetables to the local community. She is also a leader of the small group of vegetable growers trying to increase the percentage of carbon sequestered in farm soils. A higher percentage of carbon in the soil means indirectly that carbon dioxide has been removed from the air, making her business ('Sow and Grow Organics') one of the few genuinely carbon negative commercial activities in the UK. Another business with a wholly green approach is Riverford Organic Vegetables in Devon, which completely bypasses the hugely energy-intensive grocery supply chain and supplies its foods across most of England through a network of self-employed distributors. This makes its vegetables some of the lowest-carbon foods in the country.

Lessons from the growth of the Internet

What we are seeing now in the drive for greener businesses is similar to what we went through with the Internet. At first it looked as though the Web was a fad, largely unrelated to business needs. Initially, many organisations hesitated and didn't even build a place-holding website. When they eventually decided that they needed a Web presence, they put up a few pages of photographs taken from the company's brochures (often at a less-than-ideal address, if their

▶

preferred URL had already been bagged by someone else). This was the equivalent to the companies now making green gestures at the bottom of the ladder on p. 26. There was no commitment to using the Internet to build a better and more profitable business. Many of these technological tortoises have been pushed aside by new companies that use the Internet to reduce costs and simplify business processes. The arrival of companies like Amazon and eBay showed people that the Web could challenge well-established companies. They had cost structures that matched or improved upon conventional operators. These were real redesigns of business processes that gave customers what they wanted, cheaply and conveniently. The greenest companies, such as Patagonia clothing (see p. 253), are beginning to work towards the same objectives today.

In building the green company, there is always a risk that you will get ahead of your customers and that the low-carbon technologies that promise so much will under-perform. These are ever-present risks similar to those that sank many innovative Internet companies. But it is now obvious that few successful firms operate without integrating the Internet into every part of their business, whether it be customer contact, supply chain management or monitoring of industrial processes. It is at least a reasonable hypothesis that in ten years' time it will be equally transparent that the incorporation of green technology and approaches into business will be an absolute necessity. The world has burnt the best part of a billion years' accumulation of fossil fuel in less than a century – 'business as usual' is unlikely to be possible.

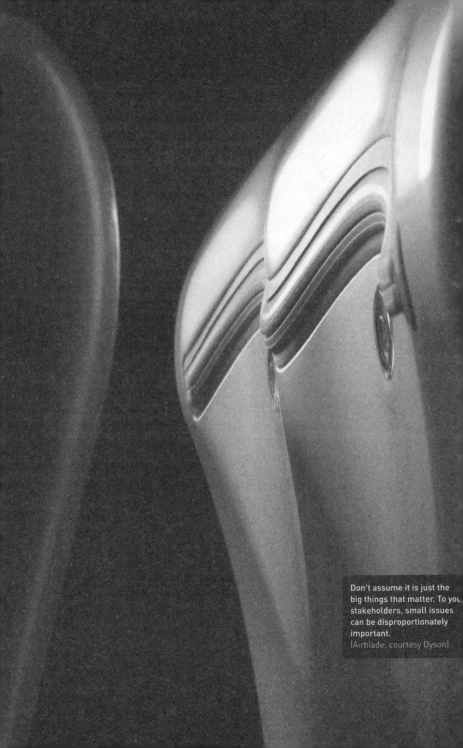

Don't assume it is just the big things that matter. To your stakeholders, small issues can be disproportionately important.
(Airblade; courtesy Dyson)

2

Know your stakeholders

It isn't just what **you** believe; it is what your customers, suppliers, investors and employees think as well

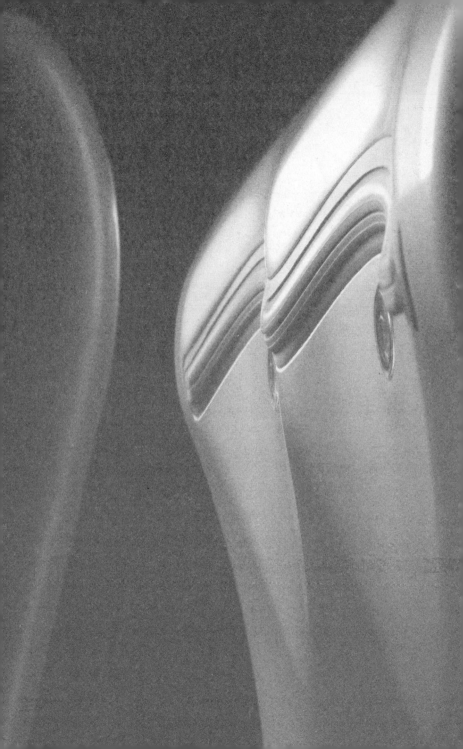

No organisation exists in a vacuum. Even if moving up the green ladder looks the right thing to do, you can only work at the speed of the companies that surround you. If your customers don't want your ultra-efficient electric cars, your new recyclable packaging or expensive alternative light bulbs, your green efforts will fail. Focusing on internal changes that don't really interest employees is a recipe for problems. And although some of your shareholders will support a costly programme to invest more in order to reduce energy use, others will complain about the impact on your short-term profitability. One of the most difficult challenges you face is moving your organisation towards a low-carbon future at a speed with which your stakeholders are comfortable. Businesses have some scope for genuine leadership, but you cannot drag your customers along at a faster pace than they are prepared to travel. This chapter looks at the constraints that a green organisation faces from customers, suppliers and employees.

What do customers really think?

To an extent that surprises me every time I come into contact with large organisations, many managers really do understand how they can and should change their enterprises to minimise greenhouse gases arising from their own operations and those of their suppliers and customers. They also grasp the imperative need to reduce the use of the world's resources. But they are often put off by the ambivalent response of their customers and other stakeholders. These people may express support for green initiatives but are then lukewarm when it comes to changing their behaviour or the things that they buy. For example, they may claim a willingness to subscribe to renewable electricity tariffs or to buy food with minimal air miles, but their actual consumption patterns may suggest a lack of real commitment to these products. Green electricity and local food are still the preferred choice of only a small percentage of UK consumers.

Consumers are not yet clearly focused on what really matters. Even the greenest households tend to have a poor sense of what a fully sustainable lifestyle would involve. Attention is directed on issues such as recycling domestic waste, but this is generally a trivial matter compared, say, to the importance of home insulation or the role of car and air transport in adding to personal carbon footprints.

Issues such as recycling are highly *salient* to consumers, who regard them as at the centre of a green lifestyle. Some of the most important examples are in the table opposite. Beside each are related issues, which are usually far more important, but which consumers are not particularly interested in.

So, for example, increasing the amount of recycling is more important to most UK citizens than simply using less in the first place. There have now been ten years of increasing public emphasis on the importance of decreasing the nation's lamentable record on tipping waste into landfill sites. But actually not buying stuff in the first place, or only purchasing from

Saliency versus importance

High consumer saliency but relatively unimportant	Low consumer saliency but much more important
Recycling	→ Using less in the first place
Standby power use of consumer electronics	→ The electricity consumed when actually in use is generally much more important
Organic food	→ Type of food eaten. Organic meat is far more climate-damaging than non-organic vegetables
Packaging	→ Energy involved in making the things that are packaged

suppliers that minimise the amount of energy or materials used, is not something that is well understood.

Although many customers are interested in green issues, the level of comprehension is quite low. The lesson for business is quite simple – accurate and powerful claims about the green credentials of your product are liable to be misunderstood and often valued far less highly than might be warranted.

Similarly, scientific issues are extremely poorly understood. If a large proportion of the UK population has no sense of what a kilowatt hour is, advertising the power consumption of a washing machine or a light bulb is almost certainly not worthwhile. Claims have to be based either on a comparison with a well-known product ('uses half the electricity of the leading brand') or by stressing the position in a league table ('rated most environmentally friendly'). People also understand the idea of energy labels, such as the ones on many electric appliances, although the information given is often misinterpreted. For example, remarkably few people understand that many products that are given A ratings use more electricity than more lowly rated items simply because they are bigger. It may, therefore, be more environmentally friendly to buy a smaller device than one that claims to be more efficient. A large, American-style fridge that is graded A for energy consumption will actually use twice as much electricity as a small refrigerator with the same rating. And the small fridge will have used far less energy to manufacture in the first place.

What about the public perception of climate change? The poor UK summer of 2008 probably encouraged the view that the risks from climate change were less than many have predicted. But don't assume that what we experience in Britain is representative of worldwide temperatures. October 2008 is a good example: England and Wales had below-average temperatures, but for the world as a whole October's land temperatures were the hottest ever recorded for that month. It is, of course, true that the UK is likely to suffer far less than some other countries from global warming. At the most selfish level, it will probably not suffer from dangerous droughts or periods of unacceptable heat – at least not for fifty years or so. So it is a substantial risk for any British business to assume that green products will automatically sell. Phil Downing of opinion pollsters Ipsos MORI surprised many commentators when he suggested that large numbers of people believed that many leading experts still questioned the existence of man-made global warming.

In 2007, he found that 56 per cent agreed at least to some extent with this view; by 2008, a similarly worded question suggested that this number had risen to 60 per cent.

Despite this scepticism, most Ipsus MORI research suggests that people do genuinely want the government to do more on climate change. In a recent survey, over two-thirds of participants said that they want more action on the subject; just 10 per cent didn't. When it comes to paying more, attitudes are a little less firm but are still strongly in favour of action. About 60 per cent of people think we should encourage more renewable energy, even if it adds to bills; 15 per cent actively disagree. But this belief that more should be done is not reflected in people's view about their community's behaviour. When asked if taking action to reduce climate change is 'the normal thing to do' in their area, only 4 per cent of people agreed strongly.

The figure for those prepared to make small changes in the things that they buy stands at 47 per cent, but just 13 per cent think that people should take 'significant and radical' steps to change their lifestyle.

Being green in a recession

Does interest in the environment fall away in an economic recession? Newspapers and commentators warn that difficult economic circumstances will curtail the growth of interest in being green. Actually, it is far more complicated than that. We need to carefully distinguish between green products and services that are luxuries and those that actually save customers money or provide people with significantly greater value. There's certainly no obvious reason why a recession

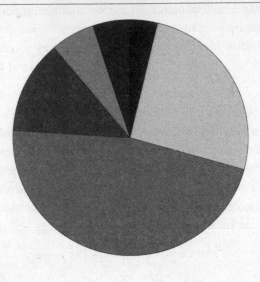

Individuals should not be expected to do anything, it is not their responsibility (4%)

Individuals should be expected to do things like recycling and turning lights off at home but no more (26%)

Individuals should be expected to do things like recycling and turning lights off at home as well as going further on some bigger actions eg in terms of what products they buy, how much they pay for things, and how much they drive and fly (47%)

Individuals should be expected to make significant and radical changes to their lifestyle in terms of the products they buy, how much they pay for things and how much they drive (13%)

There is no need to take any action – climate change is natural/humans are not having that much impact (6%)

Don't know (5%)

Base: All adults aged 15+ (1039 responses)
Percentages do not add up to 100 due to rounding

Thinking about what is reasonable to expect people to do to tackle climate change, which one of these statements best describes your opinion? Source: Ipsos MORI, 2008

should result in increased carbon dioxide emissions. When times are tougher, customers will be far more choosy about what they buy. For example, householders may well be less likely to buy expensive eco-bling, such as wind turbines or hybrid cars.

But householders will be far *more* inclined to take sensible and financially well-judged decisions to insulate the loft, travel by public transport, trade down to a smaller car or avoid going on expensive long-haul flights. If being green means wasting less, only buying what you need and saving all the energy you can, recession is good for the green cause; and the businesses that can reliably save their customers money will prosper.

September and October 2008 saw the greatest turbulence in the financial markets that the modern world has ever experienced. A period of anxious uncertainty arising from the crisis in US mortgage markets was followed by escalating financial failures and unprecedented government intervention in the workings of the banking system. By late 2008, it looked as though the UK economy had entered a severe and long-lasting recession.

But this hasn't been accompanied by any significant fall in consumers' interest in environmental matters. One market research firm has asked a regular question in its polls that gives us some interesting information about how people's attitudes towards the environment don't actually change much when faced with tougher economic circumstances. Populus, one of the UK's leading polling firms, puts the following option to its respondents:

There is lots of talk at the moment about the economy – the stock market troubles, house prices, interest rates and so on. Which of the following best describes how you would be likely to respond if you had to cut back on your consumer spending?

The two options are:

I would still try and buy the most ethical and environmentally friendly products I could – even if it meant paying a little extra.

OR

I would be more likely to buy products and services that represented the best value for money regardless of the company's ethical or environmental credentials.

The following chart shows how the percentage choosing the first of these two options has changed from around the time that the US sub-prime meltdown first became widely talked about in mid-2007.

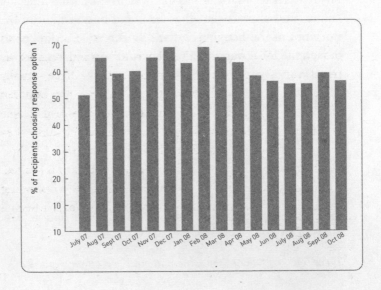

The chart shows considerable fluctuation from month to month. These variations may or may not be meaningful and we shouldn't place too much reliance on them. And whether people do actually choose the more environmentally friendly goods in front of them is an open question. However, their willingness to *say* that they are prepared to pay a bit more is substantially unchanged – over the period, still well over the half the population expressed this view.

A similar result arises when Populus asks people about flying. The pollsters regularly enquire whether people would be prepared to fly less often if there was no other way of reducing the environmental impact of air travel. This percentage has hovered between 50 and 60 per cent over the past eighteen months and now sits in the middle of this range; 54 per cent of people are willing to cut their air travel if environmentally necessary. No sign here of a decline in the level of support for green measures as recession bites.

But, of course, although it is probably imperative from a point of view of global warming that the world loses its taste for air travel, very few people – perhaps 5 per cent – have actually ceased flying. As we all know, there is a large gap between views that are offered and behaviour in the real world. People aren't entirely consistent when it comes to green issues – they recognise the problem and say that something must be done, but their own willingness to change their behaviour is limited. Although green attitudes are probably gradually becoming embedded in the community, there definitely hasn't been a revolution in behaviour.

Working out what matters

Many guides to green actions recommend that businesses and individuals take all the measures that they can. The list of options is long: companies should turn the lights off, offset their emissions, buy electric cars, reduce packaging, compost food waste, cut the energy used in production processes, help the local community, avoid air miles and ban plastic bags in the office. Not surprisingly, many business-people will recoil and decide to do nothing.

The thoughtful organisation needs help working out how it can most effectively and inexpensively make a real difference to its own carbon footprint. Focus on everything and you will focus on nothing. Even the best-resourced company or public authority needs to decide which aspects of its activities matter most and then build a plan to address these issues. Ideally, a company would decide that it could do most by redirecting its purchasing, redesigning its products or using a greener car fleet, and then construct a robust programme for introducing change.

To the rational manager, it makes sense to turn a searchlight on the most expensive, damaging or irresponsible activities. The next chapter, which focuses on measuring and monitoring your emissions, makes this point as well. But we all need to remember that organisations are collections of human beings. All of us have prejudices, preconceptions and preferences. A manufacturing company may be able to make the most difference by turning its attention to reducing the energy use of its suppliers or perhaps ensuring 100 per cent recyclability for its used products. Rationally speaking, the organisation should focus on a small number of important objectives such as these. The employees may understand the reasons for giving priority to the biggest problems, but be personally far more concerned by smaller issues. Perhaps one group gets irritated by the lights left on in the office block, another by the packaging waste in the canteen; although the carbon impact of these inefficiencies may be small by comparison to the bigger concerns that the company faces, these issues may have far more emotional significance to employees or even to customers.

The lesson from successful organisations is that keeping the focus on the big potential gains is vital, but that this emphasis needs to be married to a visible and active interest in responding to the human concerns of people in the business. However effective an organisation is at driving down energy use in its suppliers or redesigning its products for a longer life, it will still seem unresponsive and irresponsible if it does not also address those issues that most worry its closest stakeholders. Though these issues are often relatively trivial by comparison to the big environmental problems the company faces, they need to be actively addressed.

To give an example, Marks & Spencer is looking for ways to reduce the energy used by consumers when washing its clothes. The global warming impact of a new sweater is not dominated by how or where it is made, or by the weight of its packaging, but by the water temperature at which it is washed. Nevertheless, at the same time as trying to reduce the energy used in keeping clothes clean, M&S needed to actively respond to its customers' concerns about plastic carrier bags – actually a much less significant issue. The company then introduced a scheme of charging for bags.

More about the small things

People worry about the things they can see. You'll find that any business trying to be green will disproportionately have to concern itself with issues that aren't actually central to the world's environmental future. Managers in even the most sophisticated businesses can spend more time deciding whether to ditch plastic cups in favour of paper than on how to reduce air travel or whether to commission an ultra-green headquarters building.

This can seem very frustrating. One of the characteristics of good managers is that they try to teach everybody to focus on the really important questions and not to get distracted by irritating irrelevances. But for some reason this seems to break down when it comes to environmental issues. Among the many concerns that usually rise to the surface when stakeholders such as employees debate how to improve a business's green credentials is the use of packaging and disposable plastic items.

Your organisation probably faces other issues about which people feel very strongly. My recommendation is not to fight against these strongly held views. Even if you think people are concentrating on the wrong issues, it may be very destructive to your larger ambitions to oppose employees or customers. Nevertheless, it is worth looking in a little more detail as to why the attention devoted to these and similar topics is not well directed.

The use of disposable plastics

Disposable plastics often incite a deeply held antipathy from employees and diminish an organisation's green credentials in the eyes of visitors. The use of disposable plastic is a visible symbol of a society that is prodigiously wasteful in how it uses its resources; plastic coffee cups and cutlery in the canteen, and water cups made from clear polystyrene in the meeting rooms do all seem extremely profligate.

The problem is that ceramic or metal alternatives probably have a higher carbon footprint than plastic disposables. Study after study has shown that plastic utensils in business are actually energy-efficient. A small plastic container for holding water uses a tiny amount of energy to make compared to glass. The glass will last longer, but also needs to be washed at a very high temperature after every use. Almost every study shows that it makes more sense to buy disposable cups rather than their glass or china equivalents. One report said that it might take three thousand uses of a china cup before its amortised energy cost less than the plastic equivalent; that's two cups of coffee every working day for around six years.

Another piece of work suggested that a china cup typically lasted less than fifty uses before it broke or got chipped. So, strictly rationally, we shouldn't be so opposed to plastic in our catering. Of course the plastic cups should be recycled – and increasing numbers of businesses are already doing this.

So which is it better to do? Pursue the environmentally correct solution – which is probably to continue to use plastic for all hot and cold liquids – or follow what colleagues may think is the right course? My belief is that unless the consequences are expensive or dangerously environmentally destructive, an organisation needs to follow the opinions of its key stakeholders rather than fight against them. If people don't like plastic cups or plastic packaging, don't use them. It is a small price to pay (environmentally or economically) for building support among employees and customers on more important matters.

Packaging

Many consumers see the reduction of packaging as one of the top two or three environmental issues in the UK. The reality is that it really isn't very important compared to the huge challenges we face in other areas. For example, packaging is only responsible for slightly over 6 per cent of the total energy used to make a household's annual purchases. As we've already seen, the energy and greenhouse-gas emissions from food production are far more important. It would make more sense to be concerned about the emissions resulting from the use of nitrogenous fertiliser than about plastic bags, but such issues don't currently capture people's attention. Environmentally friendly farming scarcely gets a mention in the press or on television, even though it is a hundred times more important.

Let's be clear: no one denies that reducing the weight of packaging is important. Businesses do need to be concerned about ensuring that the goods they sell are not shipped in excessive amounts of plastic or cardboard packaging. But the manufacturers of packaging have no interest in using too much of their expensive raw materials, and the weight of packaging used has dipped sharply in the last few years. A glass beer bottle, for example, now weighs little more than half what it did in 2000. And a washing-up liquid container is about a third as heavy as it was in the 1970s. Small reductions in the weight of packaging of most items occur every year. Although total packaging waste has risen slightly in the last few years, this is because we are buying more goods, not because packaging is getting heavier.

Most packaging coming into your organisation can be recycled. The Advisory Committee on Packaging reports that:

- Packaging from all sources (industrial, commercial and household) is less than 3 per cent of the waste sent to landfill, measured by weight or volume
- 60 per cent of packaging from industry and households is recovered and recycled.

The packaging that comes into a business or a household usually performs a vital function. It is there to protect against damage, pilferage and contamination. Whether it is for food, stationery, computer equipment or marketing materials, it may make little sense to try to reduce the volume of packaging because the losses that would occur as a result would far outweigh the savings.

None of us likes the fact that much packaging ends up in landfill. But, perhaps surprisingly, the UK's record in recovering and reusing packaging isn't quite as bad as we sometimes think. Far more packaging is recovered and reused than even a few years ago. In 1998, the nation recycled just over a quarter of its packaging, but the figure is now over a half. This puts the UK almost half-way up the European recycling league. There's more work to be done, but tougher regulations and stronger financial incentives have boosted reuse rates in all types of packaging. Packaging from all industrial and commercial organisations still amounts to about 5 million tonnes a year, but this is only just over 1 per cent of all UK waste, and the percentage is declining.

You may find there is pressure on your organisation to use naturally biodegradable packaging, such as paper or one of the new films that break down when composted. Sandwich suppliers, for example, are increasingly required by their large customers to package their lunchtime treats in thin cardboard. Most people assume that this is better for the environment than the well-established plastic containers. Unfortunately, the reverse is probably true. The weight of the cardboard triangles is greater than the latest plastic containers of a similar size, and they almost certainly take more energy to produce. More importantly, if the small cardboard packages do end up in landfill, the consequences for global warming may be far worse than the plastic equivalent. The cardboard will slowly degrade in the landfill site, breaking down into methane and other compounds; methane is a far worse greenhouse gas than CO_2 and the overall environmental impact of using cardboard in food packaging is likely to be several-fold worse than plastic. But because cardboard is more 'natural' than plastic, many ecologically aware individuals passionately believe it is better to use it for packaging. Paradoxically, it is precisely the fact that plastic doesn't rot that makes it 'environmentally friendly' – at least it is a packaging material with vices we can understand.

Plastic 'biodegradable' film is similarly contentious. Most of the so-called degradable plastics, such as those used in some supermarket bags, will end up in landfill since few local authorities want them in their recycling bins. The absence of oxygen at the core of the rubbish pile means that the bags will eventually rot into methane rather than CO_2, with far more severe climate change consequences than conventional thin polythene bags. The 'biodegradable' films are meant to be home-compostable, but few domestic compost heaps maintain anything like a high enough temperature to break them down. Most will, therefore, eventually end up in the rubbish bin. The lesson for business is that many apparently environmentally friendly innovations do not actually result in any reduction of emissions. Although consumers and NGOs may pressure you into using these innovations, there is no guarantee that they will actually assist in the battle to create a truly green business.

Hand towels or air dryers?

Another perennial office debate is whether businesses should be using paper towels or hand dryers in washrooms. Many environmentally aware people see paper towels as wasteful and want to replace them with electrically powered dryers. In this case, a quick look at the numbers appears to suggest they are right.

You need about 30 seconds of a warm-air dryer to get your hands dry. They use a lot of electricity: about 2.5 kilowatts, or as much as a kettle. But because you don't use them for very long, the actual amount of electricity used is quite small, probably 0.02 kilowatt hours. Paper towels are more costly both in cash and carbon terms. My rough calculation suggests that the towels used in each wash required about about 0.07 kilowatt hours just to make the paper. Then there is the fact that the towels will usually end up in landfill, and will rot into methane, a potent global warming gas. Although many people do not like hand dryers, they are almost certainly better for the environment.

Dyson has recently introduced a dryer that does not heat the air but blows a very fast stream that 'wipes' the water from hands. This device typically takes only around 10 seconds to do its job, and because the air is not heated, the electricity used is far less. Dyson claims its Airblade dryers use only a quarter as much electricity as a conventional air dryer. So these machines are even better for the environment and, according to Dyson, even an Airblade that is lightly used will save £35 a year in electricity alone. One of Dyson's customers, EdF Energy, says that it used 7 million paper towels annually before it installed Airblades.

Any company moving towards a zero waste to landfill policy probably needs to install high-quality hand dryers. But is it one of the critical carbon reduction issues facing the business? Probably not. The average employee in a modern office block uses 20 kilowatt hours of electricity every day. The hand dryers, however inefficient, are unlikely to be more than quarter of a per cent of this.

Driving down energy use in your suppliers and customers

Many companies supply goods and services that themselves produce greenhouse gases. The most obvious example perhaps is the maker of domestic electric appliances. Its own emissions may be quite small, and it will buy in steel and plastic components, perhaps only performing the final assembly tasks and marketing and selling the product. If its own emissions are quite limited, does this make the company a green business? Not necessarily. If the products use unnecessary amounts of energy, then the producer must bear some part of the responsibility for this.

Large organisations are increasingly measuring and managing how much energy their customers consume when using the product. Hair shampoo manufacturers have calculated how much hot water is needed to use their products properly. Car firms know only too well what their vehicles cost to drive. The television company Sky works hard to reduce the power consumption of its set-top boxes. Partly, of course, companies make their calculations because of a rational fear that if the items they provide are seen as energy hogs they will lose market share. But there is also a secondary consideration – greenhouse-gas emissions in product use will eventually need to be reported within organisational corporate responsibility reports. Companies producing goods and services that are themselves energy-inefficient will face outside pressure to perform better. Activist investors in particular will take a very dim view of companies whose products create too many tonnes of emissions. This attitude will extend to products that cannot be recycled or which themselves embody too much energy in their manufacture.

This focus on how customers use your products is a rational one. Poor energy inefficiency of its products is one of the many reasons for the failure of the US car industry. At the other extreme, washing-powder producers know that electricity costs are likely to rise rapidly. The power used to heat water may already cost more than the powder used in the washing machine. Unless the leading producers make powders that work well at a temperature of 30 or 40 degrees, they are highly vulnerable to competitors that can promise good cleaning performance at lower temperatures. Perhaps for the first time ever, a poor record at improving the customer's ability to save energy represents a major business risk. If management doesn't focus on this, investors and external stakeholders certainly will.

What about the companies that supply you? Large companies are in a powerful position and can get their suppliers to improve their environmental performance. A nudge from a major customer will often produce more productive change than years of exhortation from government or environmental non-governmental organisations. Buried in the recent tender documents for a contract to supply a vast fleet of lease cars to the UK government were stringent requirements for low carbon emissions. Barclays selected eight of its major suppliers, accounting for 4 per cent of its UK expenditure, and held a special forum on emissions. It then worked with the suppliers to calculate how much of their greenhouse-gas output arose from the Barclays work and is now assisting these companies to cut these emissions.

The right organisational structures for a green business

Many of the people in your organisation will be extremely keen for the business to become a successful exemplar of green performance. So if your company is at all typical, these employees will probably:

- Want the organisation to carefully manage its own footprint so that it is seen as a leader in the field

- Have a passionate abhorrence of waste, possibly to an almost pathological level

- Often know a lot about ways to significantly reduce energy and resource use in the organisation.

You need to use the skills of these colleagues. It will save you money, keep these enthusiasts motivated and improve your image as a green organisation. Managing these people may sometimes be difficult; although they are usually loyal and particularly effective employees, their genuine concern for the wider environment means that they are complex individuals, sometimes with an ambivalence about their day-to-day work. Many of them would probably be prepared to take a cut in pay just to work for a greener company, either yours or a competitor's. Ideally, they would probably prefer a job in a business that didn't make washing powder or carried out financial audits. They would like to work in a position that allowed them to focus full-time on their genuine concern for environmental issues. Generally, these individuals are less interested in the pure pursuit of financial gain than many of their colleagues.

Keeping them integrated into the business while using their knowledge and commitment is a tricky challenge. One organisation I know lets the eco-enthusiasts run their own club in the office, holding meetings and making recommendations on reducing waste and energy use. But the club has no formal position, and its meetings are held outside office hours. Another organisation I have worked with has a formally convened platoon of knowledgeable people from across the business with explicit and defined responsibility for cutting carbon. It is managed by the finance director, a person known to be totally committed to environmental progress, and not just for reasons of profit. Because this group is highly visible and powerful, it can succeed in securing change. However, it encounters resistance because it does not sit within the mainstream authority structures of the organisation. Neither system is perfect.

The most effective ways of building a green organisation may include the following:

- Ensure top management is seen to be committed. That means not only that the senior people say that green issues matter, but also that their actions reflect this commitment. Evidence that this is happening could include that the video-conferencing room is used rather than travelling to face-to-face meetings, that senior management's computers are turned off when not in use, and that their office chairs are recyclable and lighting is energy-efficient.

- Rather than disrupting conventional authority structures, each manager should be given supplementary responsibilities for energy and resource reduction. Alongside other performance measures, each person should be given targets for environmental measures, such as paper use or electricity consumption.

- Make sure the people using the resources are involved in limiting them. In many organisations, energy use responsibility is held by people who do not actually control it. So, for example, the facilities manager often holds the electricity budget even though the IT head is the person who more directly determines how much electricity is used. This produces perverse incentives; the IT manager, for example, will buy cheap servers that use more electricity. In this specific case, the computer department must be allocated an electricity budget as well as a budget for capital items.

- The passionate enthusiasts dotted throughout the organisation can be used as champions for change, but they cannot always be given the power that they want to make decisions. Somewhere in your organisation will be someone who thinks that single-sided printing is a crime, and quite a severe one at that. He or she cannot be allowed to start forcing other departments to buy and use double-sided printers – this would be disruptive and probably counterproductive. My suggestion is that the energy of the passionate enthusiasts needs to be channelled into learning more about their special obsession so that they become a useful and respected resource, not a decision-maker. As an 'expert' and not as an executive, they will feel their enthusiasms and commitment are recognised and respected, but their ability to potentially damage the organisation is taken away.

These proposals should ensure that green initiatives are effective within the organisation, not simply regarded as this month's top management fad.

Companies get to understand their operations better when they measure their carbon footprint.

3

Calculating your carbon footprint

What you don't measure, you cannot manage

This chapter was largely written by Craig Simmons, technical director and co-founder of Best Foot Forward, a company that specialises in measuring the environmental impact of UK organisations. Started in 1997 and winner of the Queen's Award for Industry in 2005, Best Foot Forward is the UK's leading carbon auditor.

Measuring your carbon footprint

Improving your organisation's carbon performance can only take place once you have established exactly how your business contributes to emissions of climate-changing gases. There is an old management adage that says 'you can't manage what you don't measure'. This section provides the basic information on how to measure your greenhouse-gas emissions and gives advice on how best to report them.

Measuring your emissions does require a bit of simple mathematics. If you follow the steps below, you will find that this is only a little more complex than tallying up your bank statement. In fact, carbon accounting bears many similarities to financial accounting – as we shall see later.

First, let's cover some basics.

What is a carbon footprint?

You may well have heard people talking sheepishly about the size of their personal carbon footprint. You will probably have seen advertising campaigns imploring you to reduce yours and, if you are curious about the magnitude of your footprint (and by now you should be), you can go to websites such as www.ecologicalfootprint.com to quickly calculate it.

But what is a carbon footprint? And how can it be applied to a business? In 2007, the term 'carbon footprint' finally made it into the *Oxford English Dictionary*. It can be broadly defined as:

The total amount of direct and indirect carbon dioxide, and other greenhouse gas, emissions attributable to an activity.

An 'activity' can include just about anything, as most actions or objects associated with modern living are in turn linked to activities that require energy and are thus responsible for generating greenhouse-gas emissions at some point in their life cycle. Every time you travel, for example, you are responsible for various greenhouse-gas emissions. When you drive, fly, take a bus or train, this uses energy – in the form of petrol, diesel, kerosene or electricity (the latter is itself most often generated using gas or coal). These fuels, collectively termed fossil fuels (they were originally formed from fossilised remains), release energy and carbon-dioxide emissions when they burn.

Even if you walk or cycle, you leave a carbon footprint. Why? Well, the energy you use to walk the dog or pedal to the shops comes from the calories in your food. And, most likely, fossil fuels were used to deliver those calories to your plate. Your bicycle would also have required energy, albeit a relatively small amount, to manufacture it.

However, for organisations, the most challenging thing is deciding what to include in your footprint and what to exclude. For example, should you include the impact of commuting to work or the energy used by the supplier of your office computers? What about the food eaten at the staff canteen or the emissions from freight?

On a bank statement, it is easy to see the state of your finances as the bank has kindly collected together in one place all your credits, debits, transfers and so on. With greenhouse gases, there is no similar accounting framework, no simple way to create a 'carbon statement'. Unlike financial transactions, there are no clear boundaries to your 'carbon account'.

So where does this leave organisations wanting to measure their footprint? Luckily, there are emerging accounting guidelines, such as the international Greenhouse Gas Protocol (GHG Protocol),[1] to help businesses measure their carbon

Units of measurement

Greenhouse gas emissions are usually measured in tonnes of carbon dioxide equivalents (abbreviated to tCO_2e). One tonne of carbon dioxide (CO_2) is equal to one tonne of CO_2e, but other greenhouse gases are weighted to convert them to carbon dioxide equivalents. This is because other greenhouse gases are more potent than carbon dioxide so cannot be compared tonne for tonne. Thus, for example, one tonne of methane (CH_4), the most common greenhouse gas after carbon dioxide, is equal to 25 tCO_2e. Some gases are extremely damaging – some refrigerants, for example, are more than 10,000 times more potent per tonne than carbon dioxide.

To give you an idea of what one tonne of gas looks and feels like, it takes around 2 tonnes of gas to fill a hot air balloon. Note that 1 tonne is equal to 1,000 kilogrammes.

1 Corporate accounting and reporting guidelines originated by the World Business Council for Sustainable Development and World Resources Institute (see www.ghg-protocol.org). This formed the basis for the ISO 14064-1 standard published in 2006.

footprint, and an increasing number of professional 'carbon accountants' willing to assist.

Carbon management overview

As the graphic below reflects, measuring and managing your carbon footprint is a process of continuous improvement. You need to first establish a baseline footprint, set business goals, identify the 'quick wins', 'big hitters' and options for improvement and then put in place action plans to deliver the carbon savings.

To assess progress, the footprint should be reassessed and any feedback integrated into future action plans and appraisals.

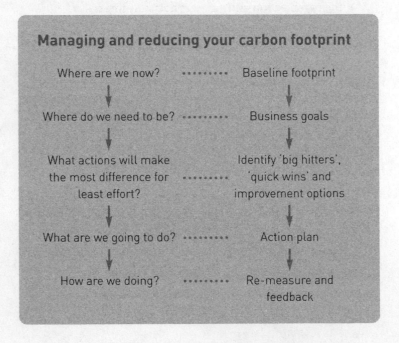

Managing and reducing your carbon footprint

Where are we now? ·········· Baseline footprint

Where do we need to be? ·········· Business goals

What actions will make the most difference for least effort? ·········· Identify 'big hitters', 'quick wins' and improvement options

What are we going to do? ·········· Action plan

How are we doing? ·········· Re-measure and feedback

The 'TRACE' accounting principles

As with financial accounting, it is important to establish some basic ground rules before producing your first, baseline carbon footprint to ensure that the results present a fair, honest and useful picture of your organisation's impact. The five underpinning accounting principles can be summarised as follows:

Transparency: Your carbon footprint analysis should be well laid out and easy to follow. The calculation method should be clearly documented along with the assumptions and data sources.

Relevance: The carbon footprint analysis must serve the needs of the organisation and support decision-making.

Accuracy: The quantification of emissions should be accurate and unbiased. Where uncertainties exist these should be clearly stated.

Consistency: A consistent approach to measurement must be used to ensure comparability over time and between analyses.

Entirety: Boundaries must be clearly defined and all relevant greenhouse-gas emission sources included.

These can most easily be remembered using the acronym 'TRACE', comprised of the first letter of each of the five principles. Putting these principles into practice is the subject of the next section – a step-by-step guide to calculating your organisation's footprint.

Calculating your baseline footprint

There are four main steps to calculating your baseline footprint (see diagram). Firstly, you must draw up clear study boundaries. Secondly, you should try and identify all likely emissions sources within these boundaries. Next, detailed data should be collected on selected sources and, finally, the greenhouse-gas emissions should be calculated using the appropriate conversion factors. These steps are described in more detail below.

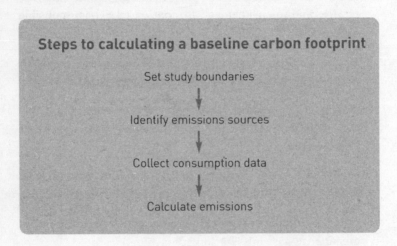

Steps to calculating a baseline carbon footprint

Set study boundaries

↓

Identify emissions sources

↓

Collect consumption data

↓

Calculate emissions

Step 1: Set study boundaries

The GHG Protocol defines the boundaries you should use when measuring the overall carbon footprint of an organisation. Although this is just one application of carbon footprinting, understanding the overall impact of your business is a good starting point. You may later decide to focus in on one aspect of your business – staff commuting or procurement, for example – but the principles for measuring these elements are similar to the calculation method described here.

Most small and medium-sized enterprises will be able to use the company's financial accounts to determine what is in and out of the footprint analysis. If your company structure is more complex – you have a parent company, franchises, subsidiaries or are part of a joint venture – then to comply with the GHG Protocol you will need to seek expert advice.

In essence, if you pay for something (energy, travel, materials, services and so on) then you are considered to be responsible for any associated emissions and should therefore consider including the item within your study boundaries.

Note that the GHG Protocol does not require you to measure everything that falls within your study boundaries. This would be very complex and time-consuming. The main items you are required to measure are the emissions from your use of gas and electricity, plus those arising from any other on-site fuel use (for example, the emissions from company-owned vehicles). However, it is strongly recommended that you try and capture all significant emissions sources. This box on emission scopes provides a fuller description.

Emission scopes

The GHG Protocol categorises emission sources into three types called Direct, Electricity Indirect and Other Indirect. These are commonly referred to as Scope 1, 2 and 3 emissions. Reporting of Scope 3 emissions is optional but ▶

strongly recommended as they can often be larger than Scopes 1 and 2 combined.

Scope 1 (Direct) emissions are those occurring on-site from company-owned or -controlled assets. This will usually include just two items; gas consumed on the premises (for example, to heat offices) and fuel used for any company vehicles. Note that any electricity that is consumed, unless it is generated on-site, is categorised as Scope 2 (Electricity Indirect).

Scope 3 (Other Indirect) emissions can include a whole range of other sources that a company may find useful to measure as part of meeting its business goals. Significant Scope 3 sources are likely to include:

● Freight transport (3rd party)

● Business travel (company-owned or -controlled vehicles)

● Waste management

● Outsourced services

● Employee commuting

● Procurement of equipment and materials

Step 2: Identify emission sources

Once you have decided which 'scopes' you are going to report, you can set about identifying all relevant emission sources. The most common emission sources are shown in the following diagram.

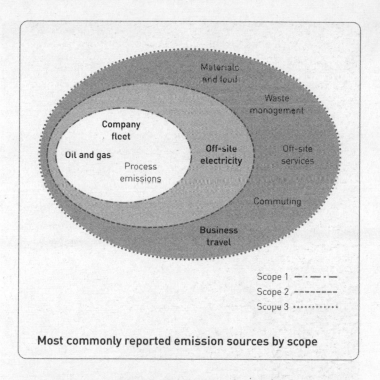

Scope 1 — · — · —
Scope 2 — — — — —
Scope 3 · · · · · · · · · · ·

Most commonly reported emission sources by scope

CASE STUDY : **Identifying emission sources**

Summertown Consulting is a small and fairly typical service-sector business with an office heated by an on-site gas boiler, an array of IT equipment and professional staff who regularly travel around the country (using their private vehicles and public transport that occasionally includes flying). What are their relevant emission sources?

The business **shall** include under Scope 1:

● All the gas used in the office heating system ▶

The business **shall** include under Scope 2:

- All the electricity used in the office (for the IT equipment, lighting, air-conditioning and so on).

The business **should** include under Scope 3:

- Staff business travel – private vehicles
- Staff business travel – train
- Staff business travel – air
- Procurement of office equipment and supplies
- Staff commuting
- Any bought-in services (for example, Internet, telephone, legal, etc.)
- Any food purchased by the company – eg coffee, biscuits or meals

Note that Scope 3 emissions reporting is optional but you should try and capture the most significant impacts (in this case the business travel).

Step 3: Collect consumption data

Having identified all the significant emission sources, specific consumption data needs to be collected for each of them. For example, you need to find out how much gas was used by your office boiler. Annual consumption data is ideal as this takes into account any seasonal variations in demand.

Finding the necessary data can sometimes be difficult. In an ideal world all the figures you need would be readily to hand in the correct units. Unfortunately, it is often difficult to find, out-of-date, in an unsuitable unit (gas is usually measured in kilowatt hours but you may also find usage reported in therms, cubic metres or even, in the case of liquid petroleum gas, litres). Do not despair. There are often ways around these problems including, as a last resort, estimating the missing data. As long as you follow the TRACE principles – making sure that any assumptions are clearly stated – then anyone reading your results is able to see any shortcomings. Identifying a data gap is, after all, a finding in itself. Where data is lacking, the aim should be to put in place systems to improve future data quality.

Consumption units

Units	Standard abbreviation	Typical use	Examples
kilowatt hours	kWh	energy consumption	gas, electricity
passenger kilometres	pkm	distance travelled by a person	train, bus and air travel
vehicle kilometres	vkm (or km)	distance travelled by a vehicle	car, lorry
tonnes/ kilogrammes	t/kg	mass of products, liquids, materials	computer, paper, coal, oil
litres	l	volume of liquids	oil, LPG, petrol

The best way to proceed is to draw up a data specification – which could be in the form of a spreadsheet – that you can complete yourself or hand on to others to complete. This is most likely going to be a team effort.

A sample data specification is given below based on the previous case study – a small consultancy company whose main impacts relate to office energy use (gas and electricity) and staff business travel. Note that, in this case, the required units have already been entered into the specification to make the data format clear (see the box on consumption units for more information). Also note the spaces to indicate the emissions scope, the data year and any necessary comments.

Sample data specification Company name: Summertown Consulting

Emission source	Consumption data	Units	Scope	Data year	Notes
Gas use – office		kWh per year			
Electricity use – office		kWh per year			
Staff business travel – private car		vkm per year			
Staff business travel – rail		pkm per year			
Staff business travel – air		pkm per year			

Step 4: Calculate emissions

Once you have collated your consumption data it is finally time to convert these results to greenhouses gases to produce a first estimate of your carbon footprint. This is achieved by simply multiplying your consumption data by the relevant conversion factor. So, to find out the greenhouse-gas emissions from, say, petrol you need to take the conversion factor for petrol (2.315 $kgCO_2$ per litre) and multiply it by the number of litres consumed. So, for 10 litres, the calculation would be:

$$10 \text{ litres} \times 2.315 \text{ kgCO}_2 \text{ per litre} = 23.15 \text{ kgCO}_2$$

The Department of Environment, Food and Rural Affairs (Defra) provides a basic set of conversion factors for Scope 1 and 2 emission sources. These include the following:

Emission source	Units	Conversion factor (kgCO$_2$ per unit)
Natural gas	kWh	0.1850
Diesel	litres	2.6300
Petrol	litres	2.3150
Electricity (UK 2006 grid average)	kWh	0.5370
Petrol car (UK average)	vkm	0.2070
Diesel car (UK average)	vkm	0.1979
Bus (UK average)	pkm	0.1073
National rail (UK average)	pkm	0.0602
Air travel – domestic (UK average)	pkm	0.1753

While these figures are a useful guide (a more detailed list can be found at www.defra.gov.uk/environment/business), for detailed analyses of Scopes 1 and 2 emissions, and for many Scope 3 calculations, you will need to seek professional advice or use an online tool. For example, your car fleet may not be made up of typical cars, in which case you may want to look up CO$_2$ figures for the relevant models.

In addition, Defra's conversion factors provide carbon-dioxide (CO$_2$) emissions only, not all greenhouse gases (CO$_2$e). This won't affect the figures for petrol or most other Scope 1 and 2 emission sources (except process emissions) but, again, Scope 3 emissions can be more complex.

CASE STUDY: Summertown Consulting's carbon footprint

We have already learned a bit about Summertown Consulting, whose main emission sources are gas, electricity and business travel (car, rail and air). Now let us quickly go through how we might calculate the company's carbon footprint. A completed table is given below.

Company name: Summertown Consulting

Emission source	Consumption data	Units	Scope	Data year	Conversion factor kgCO$_2$/unit	Carbon footprint kgCO$_2$
Gas use – office	30,000	kWh/year	1	2008	0.1850	5,550
Electricity use – office	20,000	kWh/year	2	2008	0.5370	10,740
Staff business travel – private car	50,000	vkm/year	3	2008	0.2070	10,350
Staff business travel – rail	10,000	pkm/year	3	2008	0.0602	602
Staff business travel – air	40,000	pkm/year	3	2008	0.1753	7,012
					total	34.254 tonnes

For each emission source, put the appropriate number in the new 'conversion factor' column. Refer to the list of common factors already provided. Note that implicit assumptions have been made about the type of electricity being used (that it is UK average), the make of car (again assumed to be UK average) and the type of air and rail travel. In line with the TRACE principles, these assumptions should be clearly documented. Where more information is known about the electricity, car, train and plane, then it is advisable to use more precise conversion factors – which would have to be sourced separately.

To calculate your footprint, multiply each item of consumption data by the corresponding conversion factor and place the result in the 'carbon footprint' column. Totalling up the figures in the latter provides an estimate of your carbon footprint – in this case slightly over 34 tonnes CO_2 per year.

Defining your business goals

Developing your business goals should go hand-in-hand with calculating your baseline footprint. Without an initial baseline, it is difficult to put together an achievable, practical set of business goals relating to carbon management. Conversely, without a business commitment to tackle your emissions then it is unlikely that any footprint study would be commissioned in the first place.

In reality, companies will have one, or more, business goals in mind when first measuring their footprint. For example, they may want to offset their greenhouse-gas emissions. But the organisation will need to be flexible enough to modify its thinking in response to any study findings. In this example, it may be that the footprint analysis identifies cost-effective ways of reducing the footprint that are preferable to offsetting. After an initial baseline assessment, follow-on studies may well be required to address emerging business goals or to focus on specific consumption areas. For example, Summertown

Consulting may decide to look at the carbon and financial cost of changing from private cars to low-emission company cars or encouraging greater use of the train. In the medium term, companies will want to assess the effectiveness of any measures and monitor their footprint on an on-going basis.

The box below lists some typical, high-level business goals. Start by deciding which of these applies to your footprint project and then give some thought to whether anything is missing.

Common business goals served by carbon footprinting

- Assessing the risks associated with future greenhouse gas (GHG) constraints or energy price rises
- Identifying cost-effective GHG reduction opportunities
- Setting GHG targets and measuring progress towards them
- Stakeholder reporting of GHG emissions
- Complying with certain statutory, or voluntary, GHG measurement standards or guidance
- Participating in government, or other, reporting or trading programmes
- Measuring GHG for the purpose of offsetting emissions

Your business goals will help guide your entire carbon-management process. Refer to them frequently to check that your carbon-footprint calculations are still 'fit for purpose'.

The 'Developing reduction targets' case study illustrates one example of applying business goals.

CASE STUDY: Developing reduction targets

Here's a plea that companies in the carbon auditing business often hear. 'My company wants to show its commitment to tackling climate change by setting carbon-footprint reduction targets. The only problem is we don't know what targets to set!'

Reduction targets must be both credible and achievable.

First seek professional advice on what carbon-footprint reductions are possible (including costs, implementation schedules and estimated carbon savings), then put together targets based on achieving these measures within a set time period. This will probably include an initial baseline carbon footprint. As part of this exercise you should check that the targets are consistent with the scientific consensus on what reductions are needed.

Without this final check you could end up setting yourself targets that fall far short of what the government, the leaders in your sector or the many environmental campaigning groups state are required. For example, if you plan to source 10 per cent of your energy from renewable sources by 2020 when EU regulations set a minimum of 20 per cent, then you are in danger of undermining the credibility of your targets and, by implication, the seriousness of your commitment to the environment.

Remember also that reducing your carbon footprint requires forward thinking. Individual targets should together form a 'carbon trajectory' – part of a long-term plan (perhaps to as far ahead as 2050) to reduce your emissions.

Identifying 'big hitters', 'quick wins' and improvement options

Once a baseline analysis has been completed, the results should be reviewed to identify:

- 'Big hitters' – Emission sources that are responsible for the bulk of your carbon footprint. These will not be the same for every organisation and are highly dependent on the type of business being conducted.

- 'Quick wins' – Small changes that can make an immediate and/or big difference. These are often ideas or actions that were already under consideration before the footprint assessment was started, or may have been highlighted during the analysis itself.

Targeting the easy and the important sources of emissions is an absolute priority if you want to make rapid, significant, cost-effective reductions to your carbon footprint. Although early action is important, it is worth pausing to consider any alternative options. For example, consider a footprint study of a company that finds that the carbon footprint of the printer paper it uses is a 'big hitter' and makes up more than 25 per cent of its impact. There may be more than one possible solution to reducing this component of the footprint, and it is worth considering each of these in terms of their cost, timescale, carbon impact and risk. In this case, options could include one, or more, of the following:

1 Switching to recycled paper

2 Reducing printer use

3 Reusing paper that has only been printed on one side

4 Buying a machine that allows double-sided printing

Some of these alternatives are clearly quick, inexpensive and carry a low risk (for example, switching to recycled paper). Others are more costly, time-consuming to implement and carry a certain level of risk (for example, purchasing a new double-sided printer that staff may choose not to use in the intended manner). The footprint implication of each is likely to vary depending on a range of factors: for example, the energy consumption of the different printers and the make of paper used. The point here is that the first idea you think of is not always the best.

The 'big hitters' and 'quick wins' for Summertown Consulting are shown in the box overleaf. However, carbon management is not just about these two categories of action. There are considerable benefits to be had from drawing up a proper strategy and 'action plan' that looks at both the medium and long term – much as any decent financial strategy would do.

New UK legislation in the form of the Climate Change Act sets challenging long-term targets for greenhouse-gas reduction. Few businesses will be in a position to make the necessary reductions in a single step. Managing your footprint is a process of continuous improvement. Measuring, monitoring and reducing your footprint will ensure that your business survives and thrives in a carbon-constrained world.

CASE STUDY:
Summertown Consulting's 'quick wins'

Taking the results from the previous footprint analysis and displaying them graphically allows for the instant identification of the company's 'big hitters'. In this case, business travel by private car (30 per cent) and office electricity use (31 per cent) are clearly the biggest contributors to the footprint. Travel by air (21 per cent) and office gas use (16 per cent) are also significant – certainly warranting attention – but travel by train (only 2 per cent) is insignificant.

The 'quick wins' could possibly include switching to a 'low carbon' electricity supplier, encouraging travel by train, turning off unnecessary equipment out of office hours, fitting energy-efficient light bulbs or changing company car policy.

Of course, there are many other measures that could reduce the footprint: investing in video-conferencing, switching to low-emission pool cars, insulating the office building, installing renewable energy, and so on. But these are likely to require more time to implement.

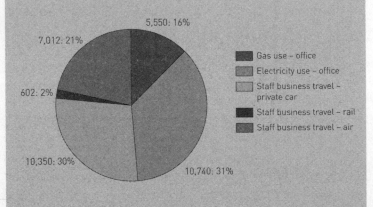

7,012: 21%

5,550: 16%

602: 2%

10,350: 30%

10,740: 31%

■ Gas use – office
▨ Electricity use – office
▨ Staff business travel – private car
■ Staff business travel – rail
▨ Staff business travel – air

Reporting your footprint

Whether you are communicating your environmental performance to investors, shareholders, customers, or your own board, it is important to align your report with the TRACE principles. Reporting should be transparent, relevant, accurate, consistent and cover the entirety of your emissions. A carbon-footprint report would typically include the following:

- Description of the study boundaries
- List of all included emission sources
- Justification of inclusion/exclusion of Scope 3 sources
- Date of study and data year (age of data)
- Data quality assessment
- Methodology description and calculation process used
- Consumption and emissions data for all sources
- Summary of results, findings and conclusions
- Information on carbon targets and performance against these
- An outline of any carbon management strategies or action plan.

Professional services and verification

If you are intending your carbon-footprint report for a public audience, you may also want to consider getting it independently verified. This will help reassure the reader of the quality of the work. Many good carbon-footprinting companies can offer you help. But how do you select an appropriate firm? Look at the companies that have been used by other people in your industry – you will benefit from the experience they gained at your competitors. Also, think about choosing a company staffed by experienced people who have done hundreds of audits – it should be able to do the work quickly and with minimum fuss and expense. It will probably also be better at explaining what it is doing, which will help ensure that your organisation takes note of its work.

Carbon-management tools

An alternative to building your own data specification and conducting a laborious carbon analysis is to use an online tool such as www.Footprinter.com. This simple-to-use calculator makes data management and reporting a lot quicker and simpler. It contains up-to-date conversion factors for all of the Scope 1, 2 and 3 emission sources that you are likely to need and allows you to explore alternative reduction options using its 'scenario' function.

This approach is not quite as robust as a full audit and may not always help you identify some of the more difficult issues in

assessing your footprint. Nevertheless, it is a quick and simple way of providing you with a good understanding of where your emissions arise.

Real-world case studies: Ofcom and Booths Supermarkets

Ofcom is the regulator for the communications industries, including television, radio, telephony and some part of the Internet market. Its main office is in central London, on the south bank of the Thames, and it has regional centres in several other parts of the country. Ofcom has about 1,000 employees, of whom about 90 per cent work in the head office.

During 2007 and early 2008, Best Foot Forward (BFF) measured the carbon footprint of the organisation. Ofcom wanted to know its carbon output in order to be able to manage it downwards. As a result of the BFF work, Ofcom is now actively engaged in detailed planning targeting to reduce its annual level of carbon-dioxide emissions by 25 per cent by 2012 and by 50 per cent by 2020. These are ambitious targets, demonstrating the organisation's degree of commitment (and perhaps suggesting a degree of indifference in the past to carbon management issues).

Ofcom's business is largely office-based, with relatively little business travel among its employees. Because it is based in central London, most of its employees have relatively long commuting distances and generally use public transport.

The total carbon footprint per employee is about 6.5 tonnes. To put this in context, the UK government's 2050 target is for total emissions per person to be less than 2.5 tonnes. So emissions from work activities alone for Ofcom's employees are well over twice what the total emissions per person will have to be in forty years' time. This gives an indication of the scale of the change that is required.

How do these 6.5 tonnes break down?

- Electricity. The average person used between 4,000–5,000 kilowatt hours of electricity in the office. This is greater than the typical UK household for 24 hours a day, but it is not atypical for modern offices. Offices use electricity for computers, lighting, other office equipment and, most importantly, for air-conditioning. Some offices also use electricity for heating, though this is very expensive in carbon terms. The carbon-dioxide emissions resulting from on-site electricity use were about 2.5 tonnes per person.

- As a government body, Ofcom has to make large amounts of information available online. Its external server farms added about half a tonne per person to the footprint of the organisation.

- Gas added a small amount to these figures.

- Business travel was about 1 tonne per person, and 95 per cent of this was from air travel, mostly short-haul. Surprisingly for an environmentally sensitive organisation, large amounts of air travel were to destinations that could be as quickly reached by train. Only 1 per cent of Ofcom's total travel footprint was from the use of cars.

- Commuting to work accounts for about three-quarters of a tonne. About half of this is from travel by rail and on the London underground.

- The next most important element in the carbon footprint is the purchase of capital equipment for the offices. This was about half a tonne per employee. In the year under investigation, Ofcom bought chillers for air-conditioning and BFF estimated the total impact from the manufacture of these items. This action, combined with the purchase of other air-conditioning equipment, was responsible for about two-thirds of the footprint from the additions of capital equipment.

- Other items total just less than 1 tonne per employee. This includes stationery, computing materials, waste and office refreshments.

One clear message comes out of all audits of office-based professional organisations: electricity use and travel dominate the footprint. Ofcom is fairly typical, with over half its carbon impact coming from power, of which about 20 per cent is the operation of power-hungry off-site data centres. Reducing electricity use and short-haul air travel are the most important priorities for lowering Ofcom's impact, and the footprint of many organisations like it.

Where is Ofcom's attention going to focus from now on? The following activities are mentioned by the regulator:

- Information systems – reducing the power consumed by IT systems
- Utilities – driving down building energy consumption
- Business travel – reducing business travel and increasing use of conferencing technology
- Commuting – increasing flexible working
- Procurement – putting in place a low-carbon procurement strategy

- Paper – further reducing paper consumption
- Waste – further reducing the volume of waste sent to landfill by encouraging more recycling.

While most office-based organisations have similar footprint issues, retailers and other businesses face very different challenges. Take the supermarket chain Booths. Small World Consulting, an associate company of Lancaster University run by Mike Berners-Lee, has been working for some time with the retailer to help it respond to climate change in a structured and systematic way. Step one was to carry out a footprint study of the whole operation, including its food-supply chains, from the field to the checkout. This gave the company an all-round understanding of where the real issues lay. Hot spots include air freight and foods grown in artificially heated environments. Tellingly, the footprint shows consumer plastic bags – though a big priority in the minds of many consumers – to be just one-thousandth of the climate impact of food transport and manufacture.

Every Booths department is now charged with finding greenhouse-gas savings, with the footprint study being used to target the effort. Analysis of greenhouse-gas production from manufacturing and transport is fed into the reviews of the major product ranges, beginning with exotic fruit, vegetables and cut flowers. Innovative refrigeration technologies are being piloted to reduce energy use and the emissions of fugitive gases. The distribution network is also being improved through measures such as increased back-loading.

Mike Berners-Lee says: 'One of the striking characteristics of Booths that becomes obvious as you work with them is that they are committed to actually dealing with the issues rather than just being seen to do so. That is how they have come to be quietly adopting such a complete and well targeted approach.'

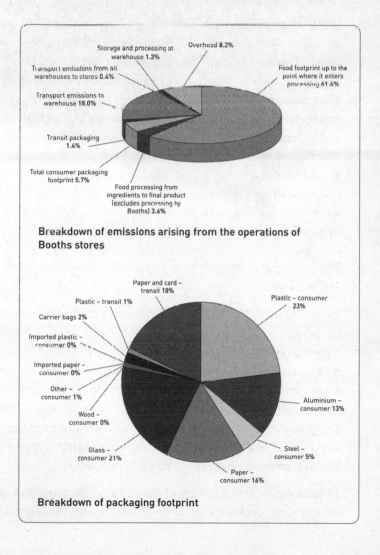

Breakdown of emissions arising from the operations of Booths stores

Breakdown of packaging footprint

Energy use in buildings

Big savings from good
housekeeping and simple
energy efficiency

Simple measures can save large fractions of gas and electricity bills. Some are obvious, like investing in motion detectors that turn lights off when there's no one in the room. But many other low-cost measures can be used by a well-run business to reduce utility costs and carbon emissions. The suggestions in this chapter can be implemented by almost every organisation, often at minimal cost.

Electricity use in business

For many service businesses, particularly those operating in air-conditioned offices, electricity use creates around a half of the total carbon footprint of the organisation. Many companies have begun to address the need to cut emissions from such things as travel and the use of paper, but relatively few understand the central importance of electricity. Figures of 6,000 kilowatt hours or more per employee are not unusual. Camelot, the lottery operator, consumed more than 10,000 kilowatt hours for every employee. This high, but by no means exceptional, figure is costing the business over £1,000 per person.

These figures mean that many professional companies will have emissions from electricity use of 2 or 3 tonnes an employee, several times the figure for a typical household. And the representative household contains more than two typical people, present for seven days a week. Business and government's wasteful use of electricity is little short of scandalous.

Where is this electricity consumed? It is difficult to generalise because it will depend on how an organisation heats and cools its building, the robustness of its policies on turning off office equipment, the age of its computing and air-conditioning equipment and whether it runs its own server farm. Nevertheless, we can offer some general rules:

- Air-conditioning will add very substantially to power consumption in all circumstances
- Office equipment, particularly desktop computers, is often responsible for a third or more of electricity use
- Lighting use is also important
- Other uses, such as office catering, tend to be much less important.

Personal computers

An old and not particularly efficient PC will use as much as 200 watts when in full use running a demanding programme such as a graphics package. Over 24 hours (in the case of a computer left on all night), this would equate to an electricity consumption of almost 5 kilowatt hours. Used five days a week, this might mean a consumption of over 1,200 kWh a year. This equates to over half a tonne of greenhouse-gas emissions per annum.

Most computers don't use quite this much power, and most are not left on all the time. But many studies have shown that many office PCs are routinely left on overnight. When not in use, most computers do not automatically enter a sleep mode that reduces their energy use to a low level. In fact, most users still leave their machines with screen savers, generally consuming at least half as much electricity as if they were working on a complicated graphics programme. So the first priority of any organisation should be to get users systematically to turn off computers when not in use, or to ensure that they enter a 'deep sleep' mode overnight. This will generally reduce electricity use to no more than a few watts per machine. In Windows XP, for example, a user can set instructions about when to put the machine into hibernation by using the Power Options settings in the Control Panel.

Computer screens are also important. In May 2007, all the PC monitors in Barclays Capital in the UK were set to enter standby mode after 15 minutes of inactivity. This reduced energy consumption and saved on the cost of air-conditioning. A year later, this initiative was expected to have reduced carbon emissions by 3,000 tonnes and saved over £1 million in energy costs.

But we also need to find ways of reducing computer power consumption when in use. As personal computers got more and more sophisticated in the 1990s and beyond, the average power consumption rose dramatically. Machines that used 50 watts were replaced by newer models that utilised twice or three times the power. The extra electricity was used to drive larger fans to cool the faster, busier processors and to power the increasingly complex electronics and peripheral devices. But in the last few years there has been little growth in the complexity or power needs of business computers. Most users only need the standard office software, and computers can become simpler, with lower running costs and using far less electricity. Most large PC manufacturers offer 'green' computers that automatically enter a low-power mode when not in use and have configured the electronics in the machine to save on electricity during operation. The UK computer company Very PC has taken this approach and driven power use out of every aspect of how its machines work.

Very PC

Very PC, a small Sheffield-based manufacturer of office computers, is setting the standard for green IT. Some enthusiastic reviewers say that the company's eponymous device has the lowest-energy-use personal computers on the market. How does it do this? Very PC has recognised some important truths:

- Laptops use far less electricity than most stand-alone machines. One way to cut power consumption in a desk computer is to copy the electronics of an efficient laptop. This means using a slower processor that takes less power and also has a much smaller need for cooling.

- A PC should be designed around the software that it is intended to use. If users are only going to use it for the Internet, a spreadsheet and word processing, the computer can be built with components that meet that need precisely. Optimising hardware in this way will both produce a cheaper computer and reduce the power that it needs to operate. If the user needs a sophisticated graphics programme that will be used to render complex drawings quickly, then he or she can be given a higher-power PC that is more suited to them. Very PC will assess an organisation's needs and set up suitable computer hardware.

- Very PCs reduce the size of components and use circuit boards with no unused electronics. This reduces the physical size of the machine and makes it less costly (and less energy- and resource-intensive) to build.

- Good-quality components – such as polymer capacitors – can improve a machine's life expectancy from the typical three years up to five

- As a result of these innovations, Very PCs claims that its machines have half the energy use of other green computers.

Very offers a five-year warranty on its PCs. The company requires that you keep your machine fully protected by anti-virus software, but otherwise the guarantee is not conditional. After three years, Very will service the computers. It says that one of the main reasons that machines fail is that the inside gets dusty. The dust covers important parts, meaning that they tend to retain heat. And overheating causes computer failure. So the company will thoroughly clean the computers and will then guarantee the machine for the final two years.

Extending the typical life of the office PC for two years is an important green innovation. It means less waste needs to be disposed of and fewer raw materials used. And, of course, it also saves money. In fact, the saving in capital costs is likely to be greater than the reduction in electricity consumption. Green thinking isn't just about reducing your energy consumption, it's also about increasing the durability of what we buy, both to reduce costs and to cut the world's consumption of natural resources.

Green PCs use less electricity. As Very PC shows, this means that the thermal stresses inside the computer are less destructive to the health and reliability of the machine. Additionally, the lower wattage used by the PCs means that the building will be cooler than it otherwise would be. Therefore the organisation will also need much less air-conditioning. It depends on how efficient your air-conditioning system is, but install very energy-efficient PCs and you might save almost as much electricity from reduced use of cooling as you save in the operation of the computers themselves.

Larger organisations should think about moving to 'dumb terminals' or 'thin clients'. Here, the users don't have a PC, but gain access to programs and data stored on a central server. The employee simply has a screen and a keyboard and a fast connection. Thin client systems, such as those provided by Citrix Systems, allow companies to avoid having one computer per staff member and instead provide a smaller number of servers on which all information is stored.

Of course, it isn't just the computers themselves. It is also important to use low-energy monitors and other peripherals. Modern flat screens are more energy-efficient than the old-fashioned CRT monitors (the ones that look like old-fashioned TVs). And external DVD drives and other forms of storage also vary considerably in the amount of power that they take from the mains.

Good printers will now operate on very small amounts of electric current when not being used. Since these devices are very rarely turned off in even the most energy-conscious office, it is important to check that they have particularly low energy consumption in standby mode. It should be possible to buy printers and photocopiers that only use a few watts when not actually producing output.

Points to look for:

- A good PC should operate at less than 60–70 watts when working on normal office activities. Does your manufacturer promise this? Can you achieve better?

- Does the computer go into a low-energy sleep mode when it is not being used? Or does a power-hungry screen saver move across the screen? Making adjustments to your computer's control-panel settings should enable you to make significant savings to energy consumption when the PC is on but idle.

- Is the office atmosphere dusty and dirty? This will reduce the life of your PCs and increase their power consumption. If components are covered in dust, they will retain their heat and the internal fan has to work harder to keep them cool.

- Do staff members turn off peripherals overnight and at weekends? Someone in your organisation should be responsible for ensuring that the business has a consistent policy that is followed by all staff members. A quick walk around the building after employees have gone home will tell you whether there are substantial savings to be made.

Data centres

Corporate data centres are consuming increasing amounts of power in every industrialised country. As Internet access becomes ubiquitous and organisations are conducting more and more of their business online, external data centres are often responsible for a significant fraction of total power use. (See the Ofcom case study on p. 83.) Indeed, data centres are now responsible for over 2 per cent of world energy consumption, and this figure is increasing rapidly.

It isn't just the cost of electricity and the carbon footprint of hundreds of servers that should be cause for concern. Managers should also be aware that many of the largest hosting facilities are in areas of limited electricity supply. In London, for example, specialist data-hosting companies are concentrated in the eastern fringes of the City and in Docklands. The huge data centres located there may not be able to get increased supplies of electric power at some point in the future. Data centres in Reading, just west of London, are already unable to get access to more electricity. So a prudent business should consider planning to avoid increasing total usage of data because of a reasonable fear that at some stage in the future it will simply be impossible to get the power to operate the extra servers.

Nevertheless, the need to accommodate increased amounts of data and improve access both to internal staff members and to customers, suppliers and other stakeholders will not diminish in the near future. Vodafone says its needs for data storage for its customers is rising by over 50 per cent a year. This means that finding ways to create increased energy efficiency in how the business runs its server farms is vitally important. This is true whether the organisation is a bank handling billions of transactions a day or a school storing its pupil records in the building and at a mirror site at a remote location. It doesn't matter if the company hosts the servers itself or relies on third parties, the simple fact is that it is getting more and more costly to handle the power needs of data storage facilities.

Power needs in a server farm come from three directions: the servers themselves, the wasted energy needed to convert the alternating current (AC) coming into direct current (DC) to operate the servers and the air-conditioning to keep them cool. Cutting the total amount of electricity used for storing and serving data is becoming an issue of central importance. Those interested in understanding the issues better should visit thegreengrid.org, the website of The Green Grid, a global consortium working on energy efficiency in data centres. But for those organisations interested in simple housekeeping measures, the following steps are vital:

- As with PCs, servers can be made more energy-efficient. High-quality components, appropriate processors and careful design mean lower energy consumption. The main manufacturers are competing hard to offer better and better power utilisation. Visit the websites of these companies and you will be bombarded with statistics about the power use of their machines and the (inevitably poorer) electricity consumption of their competitors.

- Air-conditioning. Most server rooms and data centres are very poorly laid out, and cool air is often not directed to where it is needed. Energy needs are magnified by the poor locations of the server room – one that I visited recently has south-facing glass windows. Many centres are also badly thermally insulated, meaning that much of the air-conditioning is wasted. You may need specialist advice from an energy efficiency consultant to improve this aspect of your server room.

- Next time you make a substantial investment in your server room or data centre, consider using an all-DC system. The US Lawrence Berkeley National Laboratory (LBNL) supports this approach: 'Servers and other IT products in a data centre run on low-voltage DC. The existing AC-based powering architecture in a data centre requires multiple AC-DC-AC conversion that results in an overall system efficiency of AC-DC lower than 50 per cent. A DC-based powering architecture reduces the number of conversion process and results in a better overall system efficiency.' LBNL's website has more details on this at www.hightech.lbl.gov. Although this is a US site, its recommendations will equally apply in Europe.

BT is at the forefront of the green data centre movement. It has a set of rules for running an efficient server farm, of whatever size:

- Audit carefully. Do you really need to store all the data on your servers? How much should be removed and put into permanent storage? We have got used to thinking that accessible storage is effectively free. It is not, and all organisations need to consider ways of reducing the total amount of information in data centres.

- Where possible, use fresh-air cooling. BT has been pushing equipment manufacturers to produce servers that can run at hotter temperatures. Combined with active use of fresh air, this can mean that even large data centres can run without air-conditioning for most of the year in the UK.

- BT also focuses on virtualisation, which utilises the full power of each processor. Many servers only work for a short period of time, so software that allocates processing tasks to the milliseconds when a server isn't otherwise working can help reduce the total amount of hardware in a server farm, cutting electricity and cooling needs.

● Using multiple processors in a single server will mean that work can be concentrated into a smaller number of larger pieces of hardware. All other things being equal, this will reduce total power needs.

BT claims that it has reduced power use in its data centres by nearly 60 per cent. It has had to make substantial capital investments to achieve this, but says that this expenditure generally pays for itself within 18 months.

Lighting

Lighting of non-domestic buildings is responsible for over 10 per cent of the UK's total commercial electricity use. This covers offices, hospitals and schools, as well as factories and businesses such as hotels and restaurants. There is substantial scope for reducing this percentage through the use of more efficient light bulbs, improved light fittings, intelligent control systems and increased reliance on using natural light. None of this is particularly costly.

The most obvious savings come from removing all remaining incandescent bulbs from smaller offices and other premises. Many small businesses still use these old-fashioned light bulbs and haven't replaced them with the more energy-efficient compact fluorescent bulbs. A good energy-efficient bulb will typically last for 10,000 hours of use, which is almost five years of operation if used every whole working day. A new-style

20-watt bulb is equivalent to a traditional 120-watt bulb (though some people say that the light isn't as strong). Over its five-year life, this means a saving of over £100 at current electricity prices. So although the bulb may be more expensive to buy, the economic and environment logic for immediately switching to energy-efficiency light bulbs is evident.

Larger businesses and public buildings such as hospitals are more challenging environments. They usually already use reasonably efficient fluorescent tubes, or other low-energy bulbs. Here, the greatest savings are generally to be made from the following:

- Switching from the older halophosphate tubes to newer, more energy-efficient triphospor variants. Triphosphor tubes use less electricity, give a better-quality light and also contain less mercury. They work in existing fluorescent light fittings. Though they are more expensive than traditional halophosphate tubes, the extra cost is rapidly repaid in lower electricity bills. One large general hospital has recently replaced over 13,000 older tubes to reduce its power consumption. Halophosphate tubes offer about 18 per cent more light for the same energy consumption as the traditional variety. The best efficiency is provided at a temperature of about 35 degrees centigrade inside the light fitting. Although light fittings will be hotter than the surrounding air, this is still likely to be slightly more than will generally be obtained in a UK office environment. Even so, savings will repay the investment in a few months.

- Moving from old-style T8 or T12 tubes to the new, shorter T5 type, which offers better energy consumption for each unit of light output. (Using T5 tubes with triphospor is therefore the best available choice at the moment for standard office environments.) To fit a T5 tube into a T8 fitting will require an adapter, but savings of about 20 per cent of electricity use can be obtained.

- Fitting a modern electronic ballast in all light fittings will also save electricity.

- Installing good-quality light fittings will increase the reflection of the light downwards towards the work area, meaning fewer tubes need to be used to provide sufficient illumination.

- Incorporating systems for turning off lights when an area is not in use will reduce energy costs. These can include motion detectors or simple timers that also shut off lighting at a pre-set time.

In shops and other spaces where lights are used to illuminate displays, many organisations currently use halogen bulbs. These are better than incandescent lights, but the energy saving is quite small. In these applications it may be possible to start using compact metal halide high-intensity discharge lamps, or even light-emitting diodes (LEDs, see box overleaf). Further advances in halogen bulbs will mean greater efficiency in the future.

Some places that still use old-fashioned GLS bulbs because of the attractive colour of the light – restaurants and pubs, for example – should be able to switch in the next few years to advanced, low-energy halogen bulbs and still obtain the lighting effect they need. The savings may be as much as 50 per cent of the current electricity use.

The best way of reducing lighting use is to design new buildings that increase the amount of natural light that comes into

LEDs

LEDs are now beginning to be used in homes and some offices as a replacement for energy-efficient bulbs. They are usually very expensive – prices of over £50 a bulb are still being asked for some types, though others are now as cheap as £6 or less. LEDs last even longer than compact fluorescent lights and offer better conversion of electric current into light than existing energy-efficient bulbs. A 5-watt LED may be equivalent to a 20-watt fluorescent, which means further substantial savings.

The problem at the moment is that the light produced by LEDs is not particularly attractive – it can seem slightly blue, making the area lit by the bulb look less welcoming than the warm appearance produced by traditional bulbs. It means that usage is generally limited to areas of limited public or employee use. Improvements are promised, and eventually much of our lighting will be provided by LEDs (possibly using a nascent technology called organic light-emitting diodes (OLEDs).

Because LEDs convert most electricity into light, with very little wasted heat, this can mean that buildings need more external heating in the winter. This therefore reduces the energy savings from their use (and indeed from the use of all improved lighting products). Nevertheless, there are still net savings from reducing lighting because a unit of heat generated from electricity will typically be two and a half times as carbon-intensive than if the unit is generated by gas. Of course, in the summer there will also be savings from the reduced demand on the air-conditioning system.

working areas. Good practice is now to use 'light pipes' that bring sunlight directly to desks. Or, by contrast, Nokia's drive to develop sustainable formats for its retail stores sees its new outlet in São Paulo, Brazil, use a glassed-over open green space at the back of the store to bring more daylight into the building. Obviously, this is not a viable option for most existing office buildings, but it is worthwhile examining whether you could improve natural light levels by moving furniture or partitions. Employees find natural light much better to work in, and some reports suggest that the accuracy of work is improved in this environment.

Almost every organisation can make minor, low-cost improvements to lighting use that may result in substantial savings. Small World Consulting, a specialist carbon auditor, carried out a comprehensive analysis of Lancaster University's carbon footprint and found that lighting represented about 18 per cent of all electricity consumed across the campus. Mike Berners-Lee, who did the analysis for the University, commented that:

The solutions here are not high-tech and the paybacks are fast or instantaneous; it's a question of systematically checking the campus for optimisation of lighting levels, getting the right lighting types and using good motion sensors set at the right levels.

Simple housekeeping measures to reduce electricity use

Darryl Mattocks's company makes the popular Bye Bye Standby system (www.byebyestandby.co.uk) that turns electrical equipment off when it's not in use. Customers can either buy a system that turns machines such as photocopiers and computers off at the power socket or they can install a program on the company's server that turns the devices off remotely. Darryl says that the cost of the system is as low as £60 per employee in big organisations and generally saves more than £45 a year. He said that his system works in three different ways:

- It sensitises the company to energy use. Senior managers become more aware that gas and electricity use is actually a manageable cost. A good organisation finds it really can do something about its utility bills.

- The Bye Bye Standby system can be set both to turn devices such as photocopiers off when not needed, either at the end of the day or at any time after a period of non-use.

- The system can reduce power use in a device to a sleep or deep standby level. This will generally use a couple of watts compared to perhaps 70 watts for an old computer with a screen saver.

Darryl gave me an example of a business in Swindon that had installed his system. Computers and other devices are now turned on half an hour before work starts and then safely closed down half an hour after the office closes. The equipment will even turn off lights automatically after everybody has gone home. As a result, some employees don't even know that the Bye Bye Standby system has been installed. It works entirely in the background.

Catherine Lange of Evolve Energy gave me some similar examples. She said that one of the most important things is to install high-quality meters at the start of the energy-reduction project. These will enable management to work out how and where energy is being used. Just observing energy use in this way will cut consumption by 5–10 per cent, but this benefit will slowly dissipate if management doesn't institute rules to stamp out the bad practices that have been identified. Catherine also offers a list of easy things for businesses to do to reduce their energy budget:

Change light bulbs, put timers on toilet lights, put cheap plug-in timers on printers, fax machines, computer monitors, etc. Basically, do all the things that humans avoid when we get lazy. And get boilers and air-con units serviced regularly – put it on a contract so you don't forget. To sum up, my advice is to do as many things as you can that automate energy efficiency within your company.

Useful information on how to manage energy use can be found at Evolve Energy's website (www.evolveenergy.com). The crucial point is that holding down energy use with exhortation and encouragement alone may work for a short time. But automating efficiency measures, often using very simple technologies, will usually reduce energy consumption more and will generally end up cheaper than allocating large amounts of management time to try to create behavioural change among employees.

Another good piece of advice came from a September 2008

article by Jonathan Leake of *The Sunday Times*. He looked at various buildings that were using far more energy than they were supposed to. One – Portcullis House, the office building for MPs – now uses an annual 400 kilowatt hours per square metre compared to a design specification of 90 kilowatt hours (an efficient existing building might achieve 250 kilowatt hours of electricity use). The reasons for the poor performance include unexpectedly high levels of occupancy, a proliferation of electronic equipment and longer working hours than expected for some of the staff employed in the building. Good intentions can be ruined by not understanding how buildings are actually likely to be used. The beautiful 'Gherkin' building in the City of London has proved much less energy-efficient than expected because tenants have installed partitioning that has blocked the flows of air necessary to get good temperature control.

Air-conditioning

Many businesses do not use air-conditioning, but for those that do, it makes a substantial difference to emissions as well as to electricity bills. Air-conditioning is usually installed only in larger offices but currently takes almost 15 per cent of the electricity supplied to offices and other non-residential buildings in the UK. Defra projections see electricity use by air-conditioning apparatus rising by another 60 per cent by 2020. If British summers get hotter, which is highly likely, this figure will increase even more rapidly.

It is possible for major improvements to take place in air-conditioning. Most of the energy supplied for the units is used to drive the motors that power the compressor and circulate the refrigerant. Motors can become more efficient and alternative refrigerants could be found that require less energy to compress and then move around the cooling circuit. Most current air-conditioning refrigerants are themselves extremely potent global warming gases (more detail is given on p. 111). Leaks of these gases add to the impact of cooling systems on global warming.

Efficient new air-conditioning units can achieve far better operating efficiencies than older models. Smaller units are generally more efficient than larger whole-building systems, but good new models can generally deliver about three times as much cooling power as the amount of electricity consumed. Spending more money initially on the purchase of highly efficient units – with a bigger heat exchanger and superior drive system – will generally result in much lower power costs for the same amount of cooling. The payback time will be short. However, a recent government report commented despairingly that 'purchase decisions are very rarely made on whole-life costs' but are unduly influenced by the initial price of the equipment. Some international companies do not even bother to offer their most energy-efficient models for sale in the UK because its customers are so apathetic about reducing their electricity costs.

What can businesses and other organisations do to reduce electricity use from air-conditioning?

● Running the office at slightly higher temperatures during the summer is often possible. The energy efficiency of air-conditioning declines the bigger the temperature gradient that has to be maintained, so a large fraction of total electricity can be saved by setting the controls to a higher temperature level in warm summers.

- Where appropriate, consider installing new units. Ask the air-conditioning engineer to quote for a full spectrum of products, not just the cheapest. Get estimates of the electricity cost of more efficient models and compare them to the cheaper and less effective machinery. You may well be able to financially justify the more efficient model.

- Intelligent control systems that have different target temperatures for different parts of the building may also offer savings in the long term.

- Investigate ways of introducing fresh-air cooling. Can your building be cooled overnight by taking in outside air? Is it possible to get more air flow through the building during the day, thus avoiding the need to turn the air-conditioning on?

- Reduce the heat load inside the building. Efficient computers and screens will reduce the amount of heat you have to extract.

- Improved building insulation will also help. Some buildings will benefit additionally from using solar control glazing (or solar film as a cheaper alternative).

- In the UK, good initial building design can completely remove the need for any form of mechanical air-conditioning. Can your organisation benefit from advice about renovation that would cut or completely remove the need for air-conditioning?

Refrigeration

Users of refrigeration equipment such as cabinets for retail display and commercial air-conditioning face two issues. Refrigeration units both use a large amount of electricity and also usually employ chemicals that are themselves potent global-warming gases. Together, these two impacts can mean that refrigeration is the single most important contributor to climate change from some businesses. In a large grocery store, for example, chilling and freezing food might use two-thirds of the energy in the shop, and the loss of potent warming gases from the chilling systems might be equivalent to another 20 per cent of the shop's total impact. But even in a small office, the fridge in the kitchen area might be the single most important use of energy in the company.

The global-warming impact of refrigeration and air-conditioning gases

In the earliest days of refrigeration, most chillers used carbon dioxide in the compression and expansion cycles that extract heat from the interior of refrigerators. As time went by, man-made gases almost completely replaced CO_2. These new gases could be used in lower-pressure cooling systems, meaning that the components in refrigerators and air-conditioners could be made of thinner steel. It was much cheaper to build refrigeration units that used these artificial refrigerants.

The new chemicals were eventually found to be the principal cause of ozone depletion, and they are now being phased out under international agreements. They have generally been replaced by refrigeration gases that are more ozone-friendly but have global-warming impacts many times that of CO_2. Some gases are more than a thousand times as potent at warming the earth's atmosphere as carbon dioxide. So although relatively small volumes of these gases are made, their impact on climate change is measurable – perhaps 1 or 2 per cent worldwide.

At some stage, these refrigeration gases will have to be completely replaced. The EU is banning car manufacturers from using these gases in car air-conditioning systems within a few years. Alternatives include CO_2 – which will usually require new equipment to be fitted – or new gases that mix carbon dioxide with other benign substances such as ammonia or hydrocarbons. These compounds will generally have some limited global-warming impact, but only a fraction of the extremely high levels of existing gases. Chillers using CO_2 or other benign gases will tend to have a much higher cost than refrigeration devices using traditional gases. One major user of refrigerated soft-drink cabinets says that the compressors for carbon dioxide cost 50 per cent more than the equipment for today's mainstream refrigeration gases. However, electricity use, both for CO_2 and other new hybrid gases, should be much lower. Some new gases, such as those produced by the UK's Earthcare Products, promise to reduce power consumption by over 20 per cent compared to CO_2, and far more when set against conventional refrigeration compounds. Many of the gases can be just 'dropped in' to existing refrigeration systems. (For further information, visit Earthcare's website, www.earthcareproducts.co.uk.)

Marks & Spencer has been pursuing the possibility of a mixed approach, using conventional refrigeration gases at the point in the store where cooling occurs, but then employing CO_2 to take the cold around the store. This approach avoids the high costs of investment in new and more robust compressors, and also reduces the global-warming impact of losses in the chiller circuits that take the cold to the chilled-food cabinets around the shop. This may prove to be a possible solution that marries high efficiency (in terms of cooling power delivered per kilowatt hour of electricity used) with much reduced global-warming damage from the leakage of gases.

A further issue remains. Does it makes sense to replace the potent global-warming gases if the electricity consumption of refrigeration equipment using these new compounds is far higher than in the older systems? This is a question that can only be addressed by examining the refrigerants in use, the volume of leakage into the atmosphere and the expected power consumption. In the case of chiller cabinets in grocery stores, the calculations are particularly important because of the relatively high rate of leakage of refrigerant gases. In some systems, over 20 per cent of the gas will bleed into the atmosphere every year from leaks in the pipework. (This compares with less than 1 per cent in the case of a domestic fridge.)

Business-people responsible for air-conditioning systems, large-scale refrigeration units and other chillers and freezers need to be aware of the potential global-warming impact of refrigeration gases as well as electricity consumption when looking at refurbishment or new installations. The issues involved in replacing air-conditioning systems are complex and you will need specialist help. The best firms in the industry are now sensitive to the global-warming impact of conventional refrigeration gases. When buying, you should probe as to how the products to be installed minimise electricity use and reduce the global-warming impact from leaking refrigerant gases.

Reducing energy use in refrigeration

The energy used in commercial refrigeration is estimated to be equivalent to about 5 per cent of the UK's total electricity consumption. This usage is concentrated in commercial refrigeration (such as in shops and in food manufacturing plants) and in air-conditioning apparatus. The next chapter looks at some ways of reducing energy use arising from the need to cool buildings. But in this section we will conclude with some of the best ways of cutting electricity use in refrigeration.

Most small offices have only a simple refrigerator, exactly the same as the ones used in homes. The energy efficiency of these machines has improved remarkably in the past decade; the advances in insulation and compressor efficiency have been more rapid than in any other domestic appliances. Ten years ago, a reasonably efficient fridge would have used 300 kilowatt hours or more. Now the figure should be no more than half this. It depends on how often the door is opened and whether the fridge is in a cold or warm room, but buying a new fridge may be financially worthwhile even if the old one is not particularly old. The UK has been slow to take up the most efficient fridges and German manufacturers might not even make their very best appliances available in this country. (Bosch told me that the market for super-efficient fridges in the UK was a tiny fraction of the demand in their home country – we simply care less about energy efficiency.) But if you are thinking of getting a new fridge, it is worth trying to find one of the few A++ rated models.

Those working for companies that buy bigger machines or perhaps have many chiller cabinets for use as vending machines for staff or visitors should bear the following issues in mind:

- Cabinet design. There are substantial differences in insulation standards between appliances. Compare the stated energy uses carefully – don't assume that the more expensive appliance is necessarily better. In the domestic market, the best-value Indesit models have higher energy efficiency than many more expensive brands.

- Efficient compressors and fans in commercial refrigeration will deliver major savings.

- Similarly, good control algorithms can save energy. Software that says when the machine's refrigeration cycle should turn on and off will reduce the wasted energy from having unnecessarily short on/off cycles. (This is the same with central-heating boilers – machines that turn on and off too frequently will waste up to 10 per cent or more of their energy use.)

- Similarly, large heat exchangers (like the exposed metal areas at the back of a domestic fridge) will generally offer a more efficient means of extracting the heat from a chilled cabinet than a small exchanger. Of course, they will cost more so you need to work out whether it makes financial sense to invest in one.

- Having chilled cabinets of the right size is important. All other things being equal, a large cabinet will use more energy than a small one. Could you manage with a smaller machine, perhaps by getting rid of slow-selling stock?

In addition, the power used by a fridge will depend on where it is placed. The heat needs to be able to get away from the machine easily and, ideally, it should be placed in a relatively cold area. But the thermostat of a domestic fridge will not work properly if placed in an area that is too cold. Choose a location where the air temperature doesn't fall below about 10 degrees Celsius.

Choosing an electricity supplier

Companies and public authorities frequently decide to buy electricity partly or completely from renewable sources such as wind farms and hydro-electric plants. Several information sources (www.greenelectricity.org for example) can give you information on green tariffs from the major electricity companies or smaller companies that have a high percentage of renewable energy in their mix of supply. Only one company, Good Energy (www.goodenergy.co.uk) offers 100 per cent renewable energy. It is also a strong sponsor of microgeneration technologies, and will buy any surplus from electricity you generate yourself, perhaps if you invest in a wind turbine or install solar panels on your roof. Other companies offer 'green' tariffs that offer electricity largely from renewable sources and some will pay a business for any power exported to the grid.

When discussing a switch to renewable electricity in their annual reports, many organisations present this as a reduction in their total emissions. Companies need to be aware that con siderable controversy exists on this point. The government, for example, is now saying that buying 'green' electricity may not reduce carbon emissions since the electricity generators are mandated through the Renewable Obligation scheme to produce a certain percentage of electricity from non-fossil or nuclear sources (www.defra.gov.uk/news/2008/080616a.htm).

Those who say, like Defra, that joining a renewable tariff scheme doesn't justify an organisation claiming a lower carbon footprint make the following points:

- Simply buying renewable electricity that would have been generated anyway does not reduce emissions.

- Although the total amount of renewable electricity produced in the UK is growing, it is still a small percentage of the total supply. Lack of customers is not what is holding it back. It is being obstructed by planning rules, by the problems of getting a connection from the National Grid and by the lack of easy availability of large wind turbines and other devices.

- The government publishes a figure for the average amount of CO_2 produced for every kilowatt hour of electricity that is generated. This includes electricity from renewable sources, which pulls down this average. Most organisations use the government's figure when calculating their own emissions. If companies that buy renewable energy say that this electricity has a zero carbon cost, then all the other purchasers of electricity should be using a higher figure to reflect the relative lack of renewable energy in their own purchases.

- It is, therefore, probably wrong to claim lower emissions from simply buying green electricity. But if your organisation actually develops its own wind farms, then it seems more justifiable to claim the carbon credit. You are, after all, adding to the total amount of renewable energy produced. Companies such as Ecotricity will help finance the construction of wind turbines and will provide the expertise necessary to decide whether or not the project is financially beneficial.

● Some people are even worried about this. They say that by generating your own renewable electricity you are reducing the pressure on the main electricity companies to produce more green power to meet the overall target laid down in government legislation. I think this may be a little too sceptical since the drive to increase renewables is not being held back by shortage of finance but rather by issues such as planning permission or the lack of grid connection.

Gas use for heating buildings

The gas used in service businesses is used largely to heat buildings. A small amount is also needed to heat water for washing and perhaps for cooking in the office canteen.

In modern buildings, gas consumption tends to be much less significant than electricity use. A large organisation whose people generally work in big office blocks might use as much as 5,000 kilowatt hours of electricity per person, but less than 2,000 kilowatt hours of gas. This is partly because of the heat output from office equipment – your computer's waste heat functions as a small radiator. It is also because of the high needs for power in air-conditioning systems (which are electricity-powered). Smaller offices will have a different pattern of energy use, with more gas consumption and relatively little electricity use. Gas consumption might be as high as 4,000 kilowatt hours per person in older buildings. These offices are often badly insulated and don't usually have air-conditioning, so they need more heating in winter but won't have huge power needs in summer.

One kilowatt hour of gas only produces about 40 per cent of the CO_2 of a kilowatt hour of electricity. There are two main reasons for this. First, burning gas is quite 'clean'; relatively little CO_2 is produced compared to the generating of the same amount of energy in a coal-fired power station. Second, a power station is quite inefficient – a lot of heat is wasted – whereas an office boiler may only lose 10 per cent of the heat with all the rest providing useful heating for the office. Generally, it is far better to use a new gas boiler to heat your offices than to keep the employees warm by having too many computers left on all the time. Also, it is usually, but not always, better to heat water using gas rather than electricity. An exception to this rule would be when hot water use is extremely limited and it is cheaper and more convenient to fit simple electric water-heating devices.

Let's look at the impact of gas use on an organisation's carbon output. I stress that these are estimates.

The average person uses about 6,000 kilowatt hours of gas for home heating. Electricity use per employee is higher in offices than the typical figure at home, but gas use at work is much less than domestic usage. Furthermore, gas is about a quarter of the price of electricity, and it will generally be more worthwhile to work on reducing electricity consumption first in offices. Of course, in industrial businesses that use gas for

Type of office	Gas usage per employee	Carbon-dioxide output from this gas use
Large modern offices	2,000 kilowatt hours	about 0.4 tonnes of CO_2
Older badly insulated building	4,000 kilowatt hours	about 0.8 tonnes of CO_2

manufacturing processes, the reverse is often true as the use of gas is often vastly more important than the consumption of electricity.

Nevertheless, a few simple measures in a small office may help reduce gas bills:

- Replace any central-heating boiler more than about ten years old. New condensing boilers waste far less of the heat in gas than the 25 per cent loss that you might see in a older version. A good boiler that is correctly sized for the office could allow you to make substantial savings.

- Good control systems really do matter. Is your boiler actually heating some areas too much? Putting thermostat controls in several different parts of the building can help ensure that all parts of the building run at the correct temperatures.

- Does the boiler work at weekends heating an empty office because the controls are wrongly programmed? Or does the building often seem too cold in the morning and then too hot later in the afternoon? A good heating programmer will also work out when to start the boiler in the morning. If the office is very cold, the boiler will need to start earlier, but if it fires up early every day it will waste energy. New intelligent control systems can save significant amounts of gas. For more background information go to www.warmworld.co.uk, the website of one of the main suppliers of this technology.

- Is the temperature setting too high? Cutting the thermostat settings by 1 degree can reduce gas bills by 8–10 per cent.

- Improved insulation of the building can make even greater savings. Of course, most businesses don't own the building in which they operate, so it can be difficult to improve the quality of the insulation. But it may be possible to work with the landlord to reduce energy use. It will, after all, be in the long-term interests of the building's owner to improve the fabric of the building.

Building Energy Management Systems (BEMS)

Evolve Energy offers remote monitoring of multi-site operations. For example, retail chains use the company to watch the energy performance of all their stores in real-time to detect and then rectify unusually high levels of energy use. Store management has access to charts showing expected and actual levels of energy performance.

Tesco uses Evolve to manage energy-reduction efforts in its hundreds of shops. The Tesco estate ranges in size from huge hypermarkets to neighbourhood grocery stores, and the Evolve system has to watch all these sites automatically and then alert local management when energy-use patterns appear unusual. Evolve has also rolled out energy-use reduction plans in all the different types of stores. These involve improved lighting, changes to refrigeration and ensuring that IT equipment is turned off when not in use.

Evolve says its programme has saved up to 20 per cent of a store's energy use. Ken Carter, the Tesco energy manager responsible for the project, says the payback time on the investments in new software and hardware is less than two years. He comments that the savings seem to persist in the long term and are not dissipated as managers and employees lose interest. BEMS manage and monitor energy use and can be a very valuable tool in automating energy management, particularly in large companies.

A further step that some companies should look at is working with an Energy Supply Company (ESCO). An ESCO invests its own money into energy-use improvements in a business and bills its customer an amount dependent on the cash saved each year. A good ESCO will understand the many ways in which energy use can be minimised, and because it keeps some of the cost reductions for itself, the incentives are high for it to save its customers money. ESCOs have been slow to take off in the UK, perhaps because of the difficulty of calculating the real savings. But Perpetual Energy (www.perpetualenergy.co.uk) and the London Climate Change Agency website (www.lcca.co.uk/server.php?show=nav.005003) can provide useful details of how an ESCO might work for a UK company.

Large projects can reduce energy use, and the payback often arises from improved productivity as much as low utility costs.
(A solar roof; courtesy solarcentury.com)

5

Larger-scale changes to buildings

For major investments, companies can consider having the building assessed to the BREAAM or LEED standards, and setting a target, eg to achieve an Excellent rating.

Good for people, good for profits

A large part of the electricity and gas consumption of a building is determined by how the structure was designed and built. A business can work hard to reduce energy use, but a poorly designed building will often mean that there is an irreducible amount of waste. A badly insulated glass tower block will inevitably get cold in winter and hot in summer. The *Guardian* newspaper's 1960s offices were a good example, profoundly at odds with the paper's editorial emphasis on good environmental practice. Buildings such as this will always have high energy needs, particularly for air-conditioning when the sun is high. Many buildings like this can be eco-renovated, but the cost will almost inevitably be substantial.

But it will rarely make clear financial sense to go further and knock a building down because of its poor environmental characteristics. The costs of energy are simply not high enough. Constructing a new building also has a huge environmental impact, particularly from the use of large quantities of steel and concrete. In many cases, it won't even be financially beneficial to engage in a major refurbishment. The typical business might be able to save a maximum of 3–4,000 kilowatt hours per employee – costing less than £500, or perhaps as little as 1 per cent of the average staff cost in a professional services firm. In other words, judged in terms of the financial costs and benefits, large projects to cut energy use may never make sense.

But the logic behind green buildings is actually very different. The reasons to build an energy-efficient new structure – a school, a hospital or an office – are little to do with electricity bills and much more to do with improving user productivity. The same is true with most refurbishments. Put at its bluntest, a green building may save 20–30 per cent in electricity and gas costs. This benefit, though not insignificant environmentally, is dwarfed economically by the other benefits of the best eco-buildings – such as more motivated employees, more attentive students and faster recovery in patients. How does a green building achieve these benefits? This is more of an art than a science, but the principal techniques are discussed here.

Light

Poor buildings have little natural light. Morgan Lovell, a leading UK green refurbishment company, says substantial quantities of daylight usually only get 3–4 metres into a building. This means that most standard workspaces are lit by fluorescent lights, whose brightness may or may not be appropriate to the tasks being carried out. Working in stark artificial light can be tiring. Natural light makes it easier for people to concentrate and improves their mood. And, as a side benefit, it saves electricity.

A successful green building has natural lighting in most of its areas. Where light levels would otherwise be low, sunlight is introduced by 'light pipes' and other simple techniques. A light pipe brings sunlight from an exterior surface, such as the roof, into central rooms. Another technique is called the light shelf. Fitted as a reflective horizontal shelf quite high up on a window, it will bounce light from the sun up to the ceiling. The light will then be reflected downwards again deep into the room. At the same time, glare is reduced close to the window, keeping acceptable comfort levels for the people close to the building exterior.

Good lighting improves productivity in a building. It helps people concentrate, reduces distractions and is said to improve levels of absenteeism. It isn't simply about maximising natural light levels, because this will inevitably produce areas in an office where the sun causes discomfort. Where light levels are too great, shading devices can help stop spikes in temperature and reduce glare. Perhaps it should be obvious, but businesses should also assess whether walls, ceilings and furnishings are the right colour. In an office with relatively low levels of natural light, it makes good sense to use light colours and reflective surfaces. Too many businesses add to the problems of low natural light levels by using dark and highly light-absorbent furnishings.

Also important is that individual office workers can control the light levels at their desks. People do vary in their need and desire for light, and businesses that allow individuals to set their own levels will generate improved job satisfaction and, interestingly, lower electricity bills than would otherwise be the case. Morgan Lovell says where they have a choice, employees will tend to choose lower levels of light than designers would normally allow for.

The section on good office housekeeping (see p. 101) looks at other ways of reducing the electricity consumed by lighting in an office or public building.

Air quality and temperature control

The operators of big buildings tend to have a mechanistic approach to heating and cooling: when the internal temperature drops below a certain point, the heating is turned on; when it goes too high, the air-conditioning starts up. Natural ventilation is minimised because this makes it more difficult to control the heating and cooling systems. Just one temperature is set across the entire building, meaning that some areas are bound to be too cold and others too hot.

A much better way to manage a building is to allow individuals or groups to adjust the temperature in their immediate areas. As with lighting, this will generally reduce total energy consumption. Where possible, people need to be allowed to open and close windows and change temperature settings at controls that they can operate. Where outside heat levels tend to get too high, it also makes sense to paint exterior walls with highly reflective paints and introduce dedicated shading areas.

Morgan Lovell stresses the value of increasing the greenery in and around the building. For example, a few large trees in the central courtyard of an office area can significantly reduce summer temperatures. This is partly through the effect of shading, but also because trees transpire water; this tends to decrease local temperatures because evaporation uses energy that would otherwise add to heat levels. Some buildings now use 'green' roofs (see box opposite), covering the surface with an impermeable membrane and then a thin layer of growing medium in which a type of plant called a sedum grows. Sedum is drought-, wind- and frost-resistant, and requires little maintenance. Since the plants absorb solar energy, they help to control internal temperatures. They may also reduce storm run-off during periods of intense rainfall.

Getting natural airflow through a building can also have a

Green roofs

Some green roofs are almost like private parks, with developers and building owners planting trees and shrubs on flat roofs to allow people to use the space for recreation. At the other end of the spectrum, some buildings use sedum plants on sloping roof areas. Maintenance requirements will vary greatly with the type of green roof applied. Some roofs in Germany have been left to grow wild and now resemble natural flower meadows; here, the maintenance costs are minimal. More substantial 'high-level parks' can require substantial expenditure each year.

A good green roof can have a significant effect on reducing heat gain in summer and in holding temperatures up in the colder months. Research into the actual amount likely to be saved is very limited – which is somewhat surprising given that green roofs have been in use since around the 1930s. However, anecdotal evidence is very compelling.

The biggest concentration of green roofs in the UK is probably in the Canary Wharf office development in east London. One building manager there said that the installation of a green roof had probably saved over 25 megawatt hours a year through the reduction in winter heat demand in the

▶

floor below. In the summer, the roof is no longer as absorbent of heat. One piece of research showed that green roofs could hold the temperature immediately below the planted surface to a figure far below the levels experienced just underneath a normal roof. An article in a specialist heating journal noted some remarkable results from research carried out by Nottingham Trent University:

At the mean daily air temperature of 18.4°C, the temperature below the membrane surface of an unplanted roof typically reaches 32°C compared to 17.1°C for a roof with an extensive type of green roof cover.

Just as importantly, such a roof can have greater longevity. The Living Roofs website (www.livingroofs.org) notes the following:

A green roof system protects the waterproofing membrane from climatic extremes, UV light and mechanical damage and in so doing almost doubles its life expectancy. Therefore a good-quality root-resisting waterproofing system, with a normal life expectancy when exposed to the elements of 30 years, can be expected to last up to 60 years, thus saving the client the cost of re-waterproofing during the average building's expected lifetime.

Why don't more buildings incorporate green roofs? One possible reason is that developers and building owners assume that the weight of the sedum affects the structural integrity of the office building. In most circumstances, this is not true. Not only does the top of a building generally have a very generous margin of strength but, more importantly, the green roof can be used to replace a heavier material. Many buildings use paving slabs or similar materials to weigh down the insulating membrane forming the top layer of the roof. A sedum green roof a few centimetres thick would completely remove the need for any weight to hold the insulating membrane in place.

profound effect on energy bills. Heat rises, and in summer a good office or public building will allow the hot air out through ventilation slots in the ceiling of the structure. The moving column of air also improves the quality of the atmosphere in the lower portions of the building. Of course, for many tenants and building owners it may be difficult to install the vents that allow this kind of airflow to happen. But new buildings do now increasingly reflect the fact that standard air-conditioning is a poor – and very expensive – solution.

The Savoy Hotel

While gas usage will not be the most important green issue facing the typical small company, for larger business such as hotels – which have big space- and water-heating needs – it can be absolutely crucial. For such organisations, professional help can be crucial in obtaining significant savings. In spring 2009, the Savoy Hotel will reopen after a major refurbishment costing £100m. The hotel's owners want the building to be the most environmentally responsible hotel in London. Energy management specialists Evolve were chosen to develop and implement the strategy for reducing gas and electricity use in the building. Evolve's plan included the following:

- Installing a new computerised building energy management system (BEMS) that helps control and monitor gas and electricity usage automatically.

- Incorporating controls in each room that allow the BEMS to manage electricity use (by turning everything off when the room is not occupied) and ensure it is only heated or air-conditioned when needed.

▶

- Fitting a new high-efficiency boiler.

- Recycling energy by recapturing the heat from water used in baths and washbasins.

- Recovering heat from the stale air being extracted from the building and using it to pre-heat the incoming fresh air.

- Installing a combined heat and power plant that generates electricity but also uses the waste heat to warm rooms and public areas.

Evolve expects the Savoy's energy use to be reduced by 35–40 per cent and to provide management with reliable and usable automatic reporting systems. According to the company, this will reduce the Savoy's emissions by 3,000 tonnes as well as providing far greater levels of guest comfort.

Using advanced technology to make differences in energy use

This section looks at the main ways in which better technology can be used to reduce energy use and CO_2 in the industrial and service sectors. It is not a detailed or complete list, nor does it offer enough information on which to base purchase decisions. The products discussed in this section are technically complex and a business will often need specialist help with them. Energy consultants can assist with deciding where the greatest improvements can be made.

For the biggest energy users, controlling the use of gas for heating in industrial processes will often be the single most important way of reducing CO_2 emissions. But in other companies, small and large, emphasis on careful measurement and control of heat loss and electricity use can yield substantial returns. The companies that have reported significant reductions in emissions have usually done so through working out where they were not capturing and reusing heat. The savings can be substantial. Premier Foods, the owner of many of the UK's largest food brands, says:

We have set ourselves a challenging target of achieving a 20 per cent absolute reduction in carbon (CO_2e) emissions by 2010 compared to 1990 and to show leadership nationally and internationally by aspiring to a 30 per cent reduction in carbon emissions by 2020.

We will achieve this reduction in our 'carbon footprint' by being unrelenting in the pursuit of our goal to be the most energy-efficient food manufacturer in the UK through optimising energy use and planned investment in 'state of the art' manufacturing processes, production methods and business operations.

Premier Foods will be using a large number of various energy-efficiency technologies. Some of them are briefly discussed below. Most of those listed are eligible for Enhanced Capital Allowances, a scheme that allows purchasers to write off the full cost of capital equipment against tax in the year of purchase. More details are given in the Appendix.

Air to air to energy recovery

In most buildings, waste air leaves the building without its heat being stripped from it. It makes good sense to try to capture normal exhaust air, which will be at the temperature of the building, and use it to pre-heat the incoming air. This reduces the amount of energy used for central heating. Called energy recovery, this process will occur at a 'heat exchanger', and there are three principal types in use in commercial buildings. Similar technologies used in domestic houses tend to be called 'mechanical ventilation heat recovery' systems.

Plate heat exchangers

These are sometimes called recuperators. Specialist supplier UK Exchangers Ltd offers the following description: 'Air Plates use the exhaust air to pre-heat or pre-cool the incoming supply air, without the two air streams ever mixing. The box-like construction of the heat exchanger is supplied with flanges that can be drilled through for connecting to adjacent duct-work.' About 70 per cent of the energy value of the waste heat can be captured.

Thermal wheels

A rotating wheel passes through the warm exhaust stream of air leaving the building. The wheel absorbs much of the heat and rotates into the path of the colder incoming air. It gives up much of the heat to the incoming air. UK Exchangers says that these devices can transfer an even higher fraction of the energy in the exhaust to the air entering the building.

Run-around coils

These systems have two heat exchangers, one on the inlet air and the other on the exhaust. A coil of piping containing water or glycol runs between the two exchangers. This can be used either to heat or to cool the incoming air. These coils can be retrofitted relatively easily to existing heating and ventilating systems. Putting the coils in place should offer reasonably short payback periods of as little as three years. In new installations, they can significantly reduce the peak needs for heating and cooling and thus decrease the capacity and cost of the heating and ventilating equipment.

Automated monitoring and targeting

No company completely understands its electricity and gas uses. Most small organisations get a bill every month and pay it, grumbling at the expense but unaware of what made it the size that it is. The first step to managing usage downwards is to accurately measure exactly how much electricity and other fuels your business is using. Does the business still consume a lot of energy after people have all gone home? When one machine is turned on or off, does it make a major difference to the energy consumption of the building? Is one part of the office a much greater user of energy than another apparently similar area? Answer these questions and you are beginning the process of reducing your energy usage.

The easiest way of getting information is via a 'clip-on' meter. In its simplest form, these devices clip round an electricity cable taking power into the building. The clip senses the amount of electricity being consumed from second to second. The information can be stored and then illustrated on graphs. Many households now have cheap devices that clip on to the cable as it enters the house, usually close to the electricity meter. A reading is sent from the clip to a small display unit.

This provides regularly updated figures for the electricity consumption of the house. Business clip-on meters are just enhancements of these devices, able to store and display the information that they collect.

Graphing energy use: Center Parcs

Center Parcs operates four holiday villages in the UK and is a major consumer of electricity. The four Parcs have a total of about 40 separate distribution transformers spread across the sites. At the peak of the 2004 holiday season, UK automated measurement company Sinergy Meters logged the power flows at each of the transformers. The aim was to see where electricity was being consumed and how it varied during the day. The value of this work was two-fold. Firstly, it enabled company management to see when electricity demand rose and fell so that they could ascertain what drove total needs for power. Secondly, they could put in place measures both to reduce overall usage and cut the peak power demand. Center Parcs pays both for total electricity consumption and a charge that is related to the maximum used in the billing period. Managing peak electricity needs downward therefore has substantial financial benefit.

The chart opposite shows the results from one transformer over a nine-day period. The measurements are from the swimming pool area in one Center Parc village.

As expected, the results showed heavy daytime consumption. But less predictable was the high energy use when the pool was closed to the public. Sometimes, as at point D, the electricity usage was as low as expected, but why did this level

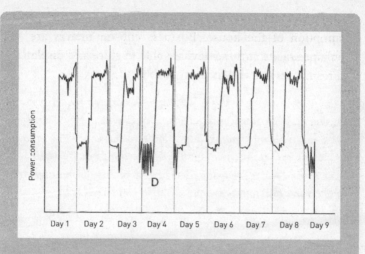

only occur for short periods and sometimes not at all? And what drove the evening peak each day? Could some of this electricity use be shaved so as to reduce the daytime peak and decrease the charges that relate to the maximum monthly use? Successful answers to these questions could save several thousand pounds a year at this one transformer alone.

Measurement of energy use in small businesses is relatively simple and can throw up unexpected results. In more complex buildings or in factories, finding the drivers of high levels of energy use is often much more difficult. Changes in gas or electricity consumption may not be precisely aligned to the time at which machines or processes are turned on or off. There may be lags or variations that disguise precisely how electricity is being used. In these circumstances, it is worth taking professional advice.

Premier Foods provides a good case study. It writes of using specialist help in measuring and reducing energy use. The company went into partnership with engineers from Nottingham University, with positive results:

The partnership gave us the services of an expert in energy management, while it allowed the School of Chemical Engineering to test out its technologies on a live, large-scale project. The innovative monitoring system allows engineers to see exactly where energy and water are being used in each of the four manufacturing centres and to target areas where it can be reduced.

Savings have come from 20–30 processes across the site, such as reducing the amount of steam consumed in cooking noodles before they go for frying. We now know exactly what's going into the factory and it's given us far more control over our processes.

Boiler equipment

In large office buildings or factories, boilers that raise steam or hot water are some of the largest users of energy. Historically, these boilers have not been managed to achieve the minimum possible use of gas or other fuel. A wide variety of different enhancements are now available to improve the efficiency of many large boiler installations. These range from units that capture waste heat and use it to pre-heat water and devices that transfer useful energy from flue gases, to technologies that enable the boiler itself to operate more efficiently. For example, automatic blowdown equipment minimises the heat loss from the siphoning of chemical impurities from the base of the boiler. Other technologies help the boiler maintain the optimum amount of oxygen inflow for the most efficient combustion.

To a small office-based business, improving the energy use of the central heating boiler may not seem the most important objective. This may be right – most smaller businesses have far more scope for reducing electricity use than the amount of gas burnt in the boiler. But when the boiler comes to be replaced, it definitely makes sense to follow the key rules:

- Buy a boiler that produces the appropriate heat for your needs. A boiler that is too big will be less efficient than a correctly sized machine – it will turn on and off too often, thereby losing heat each time.

- Consider whether you can use a biomass boiler, burning wood or other material (see p. 156).

- Investigate small combined heat and power plants, which may offer substantial savings on electricity and gas (see p. 158).

Zone controls for heating and air-conditioning

Buildings that allow users themselves to set temperatures in winter and summer invariably have lower energy use than those that do not have this capability. Giving office workers control over their working environment also seems to improve productivity and motivation. But most landlords and building occupiers ignore this and set standard temperatures across the entire building.

Individual control of energy use is best, but zone controllers are a very useful substitute – individual areas are established within a building and the controls are set to reflect the conditions in that zone. Naturally warm areas, perhaps heated by solar gain, can have their central heating system turned off while other areas are still being heated by the boiler. The Carbon Trust says that zone controllers can save up to 20 per cent of an office's energy bill.

Heating, cooling and lighting needs in each zone will vary depending on:

- The number of office workers and the number of items of IT and other equipment
- Occupancy patterns and how much the area is used
- External heat gains or losses. South-facing windows are likely to have a greater need for summer cooling and a reduced need for winter heating.

Zone controllers can work with all types of heating, cooling and lighting, including under-floor and wall-radiator heating as well as chilled water and other forms of air-conditioning. It's important to note that zone controllers can be much more flexible than simply setting temperatures on and off in a specific area. They can also:

- Detect the approximate number of people in a room and adjust the rate of heating or cooling accordingly. This might be particularly important in an infrequently used conference room, for example.
- Sense the amount of CO_2 in the air and increase the rate of air extraction if it gets too high. When large numbers of people are in a well-insulated room, the CO_2 level in the atmosphere will rise as a consequence of human breathing. A good zone controller will adjust air circulation patterns as it senses such a rise.
- Use computer intelligence to adjust the times when heating

and ventilation systems are operating. A high-quality central heating-control system 'learns' the usage patterns in a particular room or zone and starts the heating or air-conditioning at the right time each day; a very cold night, for example, will mean that the heating is started up earlier than usual.

Motors and drives

Electric motors provide the power for many aspects of UK commerce and industry. They are used in such devices as fans, pumps and compressors. Most of the motors supplied today are not used in traditional heavy industry but are incorporated into buildings to provide ventilation or heating.

Relatively few of the two million or so motors sold in the UK each year are of high efficiency. The government's Market Transformation Programme (MTP), which studies the introduction of energy-saving technology, suggests that less than a quarter of new induction motors are efficient in the use of electricity. The growth of the use of permanent magnets motors in such applications as variable-speed drives is also slower than expected. The MTP suggests that the primary reasons are two-fold. First, it is difficult to easily distinguish an energy-efficient motor from its less efficient cousin. The improvements come from the use of more appropriate steels and higher-quality rotor cages, and only an expert could distinguish good and inferior motors. Second, most purchasers are overly concerned about the initial purchase price rather than the running costs. In fact, according to the MTP, the extra cost of a good motor will usually be repaid within a year or two. It quotes the example of small industrial induction motors, which are typically about 84 per cent efficient. The best-practice machines convert about 88 per cent of the electrical energy into motion, and this difference would mean that lower electricity bills would rapidly repay the higher initial cost.

Pipework insulation

Pipework insulation is particularly important in large buildings with high heat needs such as hotels and hospitals. The Enhanced Capital Allowances scheme (see the Appendix for details) says that:

Distribution losses from a heating or cooling system can account for as much as 20 per cent of the total energy used. Insulating the pipework effectively can reduce these losses. It's also important to look out for leaks in valves and test points. These are often forgotten when insulating pipework, but can account for 5 per cent of the energy used if not properly sealed.

One large London hotel calculated that it had seven miles of pipes in its building. There is no denying that trying to insulate all of this pipework would be expensive, but it almost certainly makes good financial sense, and will be a major source of emissions reduction.

Radiant and warm-air heaters

In some buildings, it can make sense to heat areas with radiant or warm-air heaters rather than conventional central-heating systems that pipe hot water through radiators. Radiant heaters glow red, and provide heat by radiating infra-red heat to the areas that need heating rather than trying to heat the entire air space. Warm-air heaters blow air to places that need heating.

The Carbon Trust says that radiant heaters are inexpensive to run and are suited to heating areas that have:

- High roof spaces
- High heat losses through poor building fabric
- Large air-change rates
- Low occupancy (such as in warehouses, where localised or intermittent heating may be required).

A case study at the Glasgow factory of Howden Compressors showed that the cost of installing radiant heaters was about £42,000, which then saved over £10,000 a year. But since the factory had to replace its warm-air system anyway, the radiant heaters effectively paid back immediately.

Warm-air heaters, by contrast, are good for efficiently heating large open spaces, such as assembly lines or retail 'sheds'. Since almost all the energy in the fuel is transferred to the air, these devices can be better than hot-water-based central heating systems. In the words of the Carbon Trust:

Indirect-fired warm-air heating has been used to provide heating in retail spaces and factory environments for many years. It can be an efficient heating solution as long as attention is paid to minimising ventilation rates and heat losses through the building fabric, effective controls and, where appropriate, the addition of heat recovery plant and destratification fans [circulating air to stop hot air rising to the top of the building]. Most stand-alone warm-air heating units recirculate air, but indirect heating modules are intended to be incorporated within air handling units for heating fresh air.

Only the best types of warm-air heater are eligible for

Enhanced Capital Allowances. These have good controls and high efficiency in combustion.

Renewable energy installations

Businesses can install their own equipment for the generation of electricity or heat from renewable sources. There are five principal technologies that organisations can consider:

- Wind turbines
- Solar photovoltaic panels
- Solar hot water
- Ground-source and air-source heat pumps
- Space and water heating using a wood-fired boiler.

A possible fifth option to include on this list would be stationary fuel cells powered by renewable energy sources such as advanced biofuels. This is an early-stage technology but it may be available at reasonable prices by the end of 2009. In addition, for a small number of companies in suitable locations it may also be possible to get electricity from small-scale hydroelectric installations.

Wind turbines

Wind technology is maturing fast and offers a relatively cheap source of power. Many businesses have looked at putting large wind turbines on their industrial sites in order to generate competitively priced electricity. Organisations such as Michelin Tyres and Ford have large industrial-scale turbines on their premises. It is relatively easy to get planning permission, and the sites often incorporate the robust electrical connections to the grid that are needed.

Generally, some of the electricity output from the turbine is used on the site and some is exported for use elsewhere. The largest wind turbines can make even a large industrial site self-sufficient in power. At Lotus Cars in Norfolk, for example, the company produces enough surplus electricity to power 1,000 local homes as well as covering its own needs. As one of Lotus' products is the world's first electric sports car, the Tesla, this is doubly appropriate.

Wind turbines vary in size from a few hundred watts to five megawatts. The latter are the huge turbines that you see dotted over hillsides in windy areas, and these are usually too big for industrial sites. However, the Ford installation at Dagenham in Essex has two 1.8-megawatt turbines and the company intends to erect another one in 2009. The power goes to the diesel-engine factory on the site and the two windmills provide over 6,000 megawatt hours a year.

Ford's wind turbines provide what Ecotricity calls 'merchant wind' power. Ecotricity is a green electricity company and it provides the capital to buy the turbines, gets the planning permission and then operates the windmills. It sells the electricity at a preferential rate to the landowner that has provided the site. Merchant wind is clearly a very attractive option for those companies that have significant power needs and a windy site. Large wind turbines in windy areas can produce electricity at a very competitive price.

At the other end of the spectrum, some supermarkets and other shops have fitted a number of tiny wind turbines to their buildings, of the sort that are normally found on houses. The Tesco store at Wick in Scotland, for example, has six turbines from the Edinburgh wind power company Renewable Devices. These make the building look more interesting, but they won't produce very much electricity.

The typical domestic wind turbine on an office block or shop will only generate a few thousand kilowatt hours a year. The value of this is only going to be a few hundred pounds, and the cost of the installation could well be as much as ten or twenty times the yearly value of the output. Except in the windiest locations, the payback period here is going to be quite long.

In addition, most office buildings make poor sites for wind turbines. The nearby presence of other buildings makes the winds gusty and intermittent, and the wind speeds tend to be quite low. It is only at exposed sites towards the coasts that wind speeds will really be high enough to make small wind turbines attached to the buildings economic for business users.

That said, the latest small-scale wind turbines, such as those by US manufacturer Mariah Power, are relatively good at dealing with gusty and turbulent winds. Instead of the turbine being turned by the conventional three-bladed propeller, Mariah's machines rotate on a vertical axis. These types of turbines may represent better value for shop or office installation – especially if prices come down as expected.

There are also medium-sized wind turbines, which produce power at a price per kilowatt hour midway between the tiny domestic turbines and the giant industrial machines. These windmills might be erected in the grounds of an office building. The Scottish firm Proven makes machines that range in size up to 15 kilowatts. These will generate as much as 30,000 kilowatt hours per year in the best locations, but they can cost £40,000, or even more. In addition, they need their own steel towers, and the work needed to securely anchor them into the ground can sometimes be very expensive.

An organisation contemplating installing a wind turbine on its own needs to do a relatively complex set of calculations to work out whether it will be cost-effective:

- Install a wind-speed measurement device at the site. This will be on a pole and should be set at the same height as the nacelle of the turbine. The amount of electricity generated by a turbine depends critically on typical wind speeds, so it is vitally important that this measurement is accurate. You will probably need professional help, and may even need planning permission just for the anemometer. Garrad Hassan is one of the specialist consultancies operating in this area and can offer wind measurement services for large potential projects. (See www.garradhassan.com for more information.)

- The usable power in the wind rises with the cube of the wind speed; for example, a gust of 20 miles an hour has eight times as much energy as one of 10 mph. So the wind speed measurement needs to record both the arithmetic average velocity and also the typical distribution of the speeds. In order to get accurate records, the anemometer needs to take measurements for a substantial period of time.

- A range of manufacturers should be approached and asked

to provide assessments of how much electricity is likely to be produced under typical conditions at your site. Some turbines work well at low wind speeds, while other manufacturers have focused on building windmills that operate best in high winds.

- Now will be the time to get a detailed quotation for the price of the turbines that appear to be best suited to your site.

- You will then need to estimate how much of your electricity output will be used on your premises and how much will be exported. If all the power is used your side of the meter, it is easy to calculate how much is saved – just deduce the amount from your electricity bill. In most circumstances, however, you will sometimes be exporting power rather than using it in your organisation. So you need to know what the electricity companies will pay you for the power that spills back on to the local grid. This figure will be a lot less than the price you pay for your own power.

- As well as the savings arising from the reduced power purchases and the cash generated from electricity exported outside the business, you will benefit from Renewable Obligation Certificates (ROCs). For every megawatt hour of power you generate, you will be entitled to one ROC. ROCs can be sold on – their current open market price is about £50, though this figure can fluctuate sharply. (Note, however, that if you sell the ROCs, you may not be able to legitimately claim that the turbines are reducing your carbon footprint, since the buyer of the certificates would be an electricity company doing so to avoid having to build renewable capacity itself.)

Broadly speaking, a business using almost all of the power itself will probably find that a mid-size turbine (like the Proven 15-kilowatt machine) will pay for itself in eight or nine years. This is based on current electricity prices; if prices fall, then payback is delayed. In addition, larger machines will deliver better returns.

The alternative is get an intermediary, such as Ecotricity, to build the turbine for you. Ecotricity will be taking the risks and your return will come from the reduced prices for electricity generated by the turbines installed on your premises.

Solar photovoltaic panels

Solar photovoltaics (solar PV or just PV) are solar panels that create electricity. At present, this is an expensive technology and, except perhaps along the sunny south coast of the UK, it makes little direct financial sense to put PV panels on an office or factory roof. This will probably change over the next decade as panels become cheaper.

Solar PV installations are usually installed on building roofs. Facing south, the panels are placed so as to capture as much sunlight as possible. They turn the energy in light into electricity and are used to replace some of an organisation's need for power from the grid. The size of PV installations is usually expressed in terms of the peak electricity output in midday summer sun. To get one kilowatt of power requires something over six square metres of PV panels. So, the amount of electricity you can generate depends on the size of the roof you have available.

A one-kilowatt installation facing due south will deliver about

1,000 kilowatt hours in a sunny location in the south west of England. The further north you go, the smaller the amount of power that is generated.

Given that one kilowatt of peak power will probably cost about £5,000, the economics look poor. If all the 1,000 kilowatt hours replace electricity bought from the grid, and none is exported, the total saving will only be £100 if electricity costs 10p a kilowatt hour. Even when you factor in the Renewable Obligation Certificate (worth around £50) available for every 500 kilowatt hours of energy produced, the cash return is less than 5 per cent on the investment. So, if electricity and ROC prices stay the same, the payback time will be more than twenty years – and even more in northern Britain.

That said, for schools and not-for-profit organisations there may be some substantial subsidies available. In some cases, these may reduce the cost to zero. But for other businesses, photovoltaics remain expensive, not least because the UK is not the best place to capture solar energy.

It makes more sense to plan to install PV panels in a few years' time. Solar-panel prices are currently high because of a world-wide shortage of pure silicon, but this is likely to abate during 2009. Technology is also moving extremely rapidly; we may see huge reductions in the cost of panels over the next few years. So, although solar panels are a visible symbol of an organisation's commitment to being green, it is almost certainly better to wait rather than buy PV today.

Solar hot water

This is a much cheaper technology than PV. In its very simplest form, a flat plate on a roof collects solar energy and uses it to heat hot water. More complicated installations use vacuum tubes to heat a liquid, which then passes through a heat exchanger and heats the water in a tank. Solar collectors can provide an organisation's needs for washbasins, showers or kitchen dish-washing.

If it's easy to plumb the pipes to take the hot water from the roof to a storage tank, then a solar water system will probably save your business money. The savings won't be huge – not least because most companies use relatively little hot water – but it makes sense to employ this green technology where you can. In domestic installations in the south of Britain, payback times are probably ten years or more, but larger commercial systems are likely to offer a slightly better return.

Ground-source heat pumps

Heat pumps can be thought of as refrigerators in reverse. A fridge cools the air inside it, while the compressor on the back gets hot. A heat pump generally heats air or water inside a building by taking warmth from the ground or the air and transferring it into the structure. This is not a 'free' process – both types of heat transfer need electricity to operate. But the amount of energy needed to operate a heat pump is usually only one quarter or less of the amount of heat that is transferred from one area to another. So it can represent a cost-effective way of heating (or cooling) a building.

A ground-source heat pump has three principal components:

- A loop of pipe, either horizontal and buried a few metres into the ground or vertical going perhaps 100 metres down in a borehole. The loop is usually a closed circuit and is filled with water and liquids to stop it freezing. Where there is a suitable aquifer underneath the building, it may be possible to use an open circuit, which uses the water and then returns it to the aquifer.

- The heat pump itself. The temperature a few metres under the surface tends to match the average temperature during the year. So in winter in the UK, the below-ground temperature is about 10 degrees Celsius. In winter, this is much higher than the average air temperature, and the heat pump can be used to magnify this difference. Much as in a domestic fridge, the pump consists of an evaporator, a compressor and a condenser. In summer, the heating process works in reverse.

- A circuit, which takes the heat around the building. This functions in the same way as an ordinary domestic hot-water circuit for heating radiators.

Heat pumps are mostly used in new buildings or where an entire system has to be replaced. They must be correctly designed and very carefully sized in order to provide the correct amount of heating and cooling in winter. The efficiency of a heat pump will vary according to the temperature gradient that is required. Taking 10-degree water up to 60 degrees or even more is possible, but requires proportionately more external energy than increasing the temperature to only 30 degrees. The best efficiencies are gained when large amounts of relatively cool water flow around an under-floor heating system rather than small amounts of very hot water through narrow-bored pipes, as would be the case in most domestic central-heating systems for example. Open-plan offices are particularly effectively heated by water from such a system.

The head office of the Chelsea Building Society is a good example of an installation that uses vertical boreholes. Completed in 2006, this new office building is heated and cooled by 108 boreholes sunk almost 100 metres into the ground. By contrast, a system installed by the same company – Geothermal International – at the Solihull Inclusive Learning Centre in 2008 employs 54 horizontal trenches 100 metres long leading away from the building. (For more details, visit www.geoheat.co.uk.)

The installation costs of a ground-source heat pump will be higher than a conventional boiler and radiator system for a commercial or public building. The extra cost will be recouped over several years by reduced heating bills. Ground-source heat pumps are therefore appropriate investments for ESCOs (see p. 122). The other reason why new buildings use heat pumps is that this approach to heating meets the requirements of council planners for low-carbon buildings. So, obtaining planning permission is much easier if heat pumps are specified in the application.

In most circumstances, using a heat pump will reduce carbon emissions because the electricity needed for the operation of the pump will have a smaller carbon footprint than the gas heating that it substitutes. Of course, the system can be made entirely carbon neutral by powering the pump with wind turbines or solar PV, though this will substantially increase the cost of the system.

Replacing air-conditioning

Glaxo Smith Kline's (GSK) west London headquarters uses water from the nearby Grand Union Canal to help cool the building in summer. The water is taken from the canal and passed through a heat exchanger, where it pre-chills the fresh air that is going into the building. The water, slightly warmed by the process, is then returned to the canal. Up to 2.4 million litres are taken out of the canal and returned each working day. The scheme replaces a traditional air-conditioning system and is primarily used to cool the company's server farm. This installation isn't using heat-pump technology, but rather a simple heat exchanger, which relies on the fact the canal water will tend to be considerably colder than air temperatures in summer.

GSK indicates that the cost of the system is about £500,000. At the electricity prices of late 2008, the savings are more than £100,000, so GSK says that the payback is less than five years. The owner of the network, British Waterways, thinks that a thousand other buildings could use canal water to provide summer cooling.

Space and water heating using a wood-fired boiler

Heating using wood or 'biomass' is becoming increasingly popular, with some boilers now able to use wood chips or compressed-wood pellets. Wood-chip heating, particularly in areas where forest residues are cheaply available, can be broadly competitive with gas central heating. Though it is not as convenient – wood chips need to be delivered regularly and reliably – the cost per kilowatt hour of heat can be much the same as in other systems. The best systems, such as the one installed in the Forestry Commission offices at Smithtown in Scotland, have an underground store into which lorries can tip the wood chips. An automatic feeder then takes the wood upwards into the boiler. Stuart Major of Oxfordshire Wood Heat took me to see a new installation of an Austrian wood-chip boiler on an estate in the Chilterns, near Reading. Depressed prices for the local woods mean that timber has virtually no value and can be productively used in efficient wood boilers such as those installed by his company (see www.oxonwoodheat.com).

Central-heating systems using wood pellets are even easier to use. Fully automatic boilers can feed the right quantity of pellets into the burning chamber as and when needed. Pellet boilers are also extremely efficient, capturing as much as 90 per cent of the heating value of the wood. Every few weeks, a small quantity of ash will need to be removed from the combustion area, but otherwise the boiler can operate unattended – it can be run on a timer and controlled from a thermostat.

Businesses installing wood-pellet boilers qualify for Enhanced Capital Allowances (see the Appendix for more details). This partly compensates for the higher capital cost of installing these machines than a conventional condensing boiler.

In terms of carbon emissions, wood-based fuel produces CO_2 when it's burned, but no more than the amount it soaked up from the atmosphere by the tree as it grew. As long as the wood comes from well-managed sources, its carbon footprint is very small, consisting only of the energy used to harvest and transport it.

Using a wood-pellet stove

Like domestic homes, offices and other buildings can use wood-pellet heating stoves. They are attractive to look at – often with a glass window through which one can see cheering flames – and can make public rooms more appealing to be in. The National Energy Foundation near Milton Keynes is a charity that supports the growth of renewable energy. It bought a wood-pellet stove to heat its main conference room. The model it chose – the Enviro Evolution – has an output of up to 8 kilowatt hours and can heat a well-insulated room of 150 square metres (approximately 50 by 30 feet). The stove has a 39-kg hopper that can be easily filled with pellets; an auger silently transfers the pellets into the stove.

Staff at the National Energy Foundation are pleased with the stove. One staff member said: 'The system is surprisingly compact for the amount of heat it produces. Visitors are amazed when they feel how much heat is generated.' The stove cost less than £1,500 from a supplier in Wales, and pellets are bought from a local supplier. The price of pellets will vary across the UK, depending partly on the local availability of wood and partly on the distance they have to be transported. But everywhere in the UK can get pellets for less than 5p a kilowatt hour, and in the best locations they cost less than 3p, or less than the price of mains gas.

Combined heat and power

Most offices are heated by gas and powered by electricity. The electricity is generated in large and fairly inefficient power stations. Further inefficiency is caused by power losses in the electricity transmission network. Large-scale power plants also produce large amounts of waste heat. A combined heat and power (CHP) plant avoids most of this waste by generating electricity locally, usually close to the building that uses the power, and utilising the otherwise wasted heat for central heating and hot water, or even to operate chillers for cooling in summer.

Although CHP may offer substantial savings in terms of carbon emissions – largely by using heat that would otherwise be emitted to the atmosphere from cooling towers – most examples are not 'renewable', as they are powered by mains gas. It is, though, possible to run a CHP plant on renewable wood.

CHP is usually best employed in industrial installations that have a high and continuous need for heat; examples include chemical plants, some food-processing companies and paper mills. The electricity may be used on the site or may be exported to the national grid. Some smaller buildings also find it economic to use packaged CHP plants to provide heat and cooling as required, generating electricity at the same time. Typical users are leisure facilities, hospitals and even some offices.

However, UK companies have never been enthusiastic users of CHP, largely because the cost savings have been difficult to accurately predict. Swings in gas and electricity prices make the financial case for CHP harder to pin down. Of the 1,500 or so commercial CHP installations in the UK, about 1,000 are used to heat buildings rather than drive industrial processes. However, most of these are quite small and the amount of

Tesco's use of CHP

In December 2008, Tesco announced a plan to put combined heat and power plants at another fifty of its stores. The CHP installations will reduce emissions by about 10 per cent at each store. Most will run on gas from the mains, but one pioneering plant will be fuelled by biodiesel. Lucy Neville Rolfe of Tesco said:

Our trials have shown us that this is a much more efficient way to create electricity so it makes sense – both financially and environmentally – for us to put our full weight behind it. We expect our investments in CHP to have paid back within eight years and, as the technology is refined and the market matures, this will come down further still.

Tesco is using conventional small-scale CHP plants with an electrical efficiency of about 32 per cent. Another 50 per cent of the energy from the combustion is captured as useful heat for the store. At one plant, the heat from the CHP engine will be used to drive a machine for producing chilled water to cool the store.

electricity generated is a tiny fraction of that produced by the large industrial CHP generators located in places such as oil refineries.

Within the next five to ten years, we may see CHP revitalised, possibly by new technologies that increase the amount of electricity that can be generated per unit of fuel used. Fuel cells – such as the proposed solid-oxide cell from Rolls-Royce – will make generating electricity much more financially attractive (see www.energy.rolls-royce.com/Solid-Oxide-Fuel-Cells for more information). In addition, it may be possible to move from gas and diesel as the primary source of energy to renewable fuels such as second-generation biofuels (see p. 180).

CHP equipment can also be eligible for Enhanced Capital Allowances (see Appendix).

THE ZERO EMIS

ELEC

⑤ SMITH
ELECTRIC VEHICLES

Much travel is unnecessary o
expensive. Technology and g
management can cut your bil
(Smith electric van; courtesy
Smith)

6

Travel and transport

Reducing emissions on the road and in the air

No business can avoid travel – every firm needs to meet customers, negotiate with suppliers and travel to business conferences. And, of course, goods need to get from A to B. But it's still possible to make fuel and emissions savings in several areas. You can focus your company policy on buying low-emissions vehicles, and then maintain them properly to help keep fuel consumption down. Staff can be taught how to drive efficiently, and Internet-based collaboration tools offer real potential for reducing the amount of travel by air. All of these strategies should also make your business greener and more productive.

Making savings on the road

Private cars are responsible for about 12 per cent of the UK's greenhouse-gas emissions. Probably about a third comes from business mileage. Commercial vehicles, such as vans and heavy lorries, add another 8 per cent or so to emissions. This chapter looks at how organisations can reduce the climate change impact of their business mileage. It mainly focuses on cars and vans, but many of the same lessons also apply to larger commercial vehicles.

An employee driving 25,000 miles in a typical company car will burn enough fuel to produce over 6 tonnes of CO_2 emissions a year. The petrol will cost about £3,500 a year (at 90p a litre). Getting on top of emissions from your vehicles makes good financial sense, whether your fleet consists of one car or a thousand vehicles.

You can help reduce emissions and the cost of running your vehicles in three main ways:

- Changing to more efficient vehicles
- Driving better
- Driving less.

Each of these choices offers fleet operators and individual drivers large scope for savings in cash and reductions in greenhouse-gas emissions. How much difference can a committed effort make? Large companies offer impressive success stories. BT, for example, has reduced its fleet emissions from 186,000 tonnes to 125,000 tonnes in the last eleven years, a cut of about a third. Big changes include a gradual reduction in the use of inefficient petrol-engined company cars and limiting vehicle speeds to avoid excessive fuel consumption. Many other organisations have achieved significant reductions, though rarely as much as BT.

Though there's still a long way to go, vehicles are generally becoming more efficient. According to the Society of Motor Manufacturers and Traders (SMMT), the trade body for the car industry, CO_2 emissions from the average new car work out at around 165 grammes per kilometre. This figure has been falling by between 1 and 1½ per cent each year. Perhaps surprisingly, the figure for new business cars is now slightly lower than this, presumably because the taxation of business cars has become increasingly punitive, pushing fleet buyers towards lower-emission models.

To be totally clear, the amount of petrol or diesel a vehicle uses is directly proportional to the CO_2 it produces. There are very slight variations between types of petrol but, broadly speaking, each litre will produce about 2.3 kilogrammes of CO_2 when burnt. The figure for diesel is slightly higher. So, if you buy a car, van or lorry with better fuel consumption, all other things being equal you will reduce the emissions proportionately.

Choosing vehicles and fuels

Let's take a look at the various green options available to fleet managers – from diesels and hybrids through to electric vans and vehicles powered by liquefied petroleum gas (LPG).

Switching to diesel

Most fleet operators will be aware that the single most important change that they can make is to switch from petrol to diesel cars. A litre of diesel is heavier than petrol and produces almost a tenth more CO_2 when combusted in an engine. Nevertheless, diesel cars are usually more than 15 per cent better in terms of CO_2 emissions than their direct petrol equivalents. This is principally because the combustion cycle wastes less of the energy than its petrol equivalent. Diesel cars use far fewer litres of fuel than equivalent petrol models. So, although diesel fuel is more expensive to buy in the UK, it still makes financial sense to switch from petrol.

Here are two examples of the emissions performance of two pairs of comparable cars:

BMW 3 series saloon

318I (petrol)	142 grammes per kilometre
318d (diesel)	123 grammes per kilometre
Saving	Over 13 per cent

Peugeot 207 (supermini)

1.4 (95 bhp, petrol)	145 grammes per kilometre
1.4 HDI (90 bhp, diesel)	120 grammes per kilometre
Saving	Over 17 per cent

The UK woke up late to the emissions advantages of using diesel. Only 40 per cent of new cars in Britain are diesel-powered compared to 70 per cent in France. The UK has one of the lowest shares of diesel engines in Europe, partly because other countries use fuel tax rates to give an advantage to diesel fuel and partly because the purchase price of diesel cars has been somewhat higher.

Many fleets are stuck with relatively inefficient petrol vehicles. One large communications company has petrol cars with typical emissions 30 grammes per kilometre higher than its diesel fleet. So, a driver of a petrol car may emit more than a tonne more CO_2 each year than a typical diesel car user.

Smaller cars

Few things will have as much effect on your company's road

emissions as persuading your drivers to use smaller cars. The very best smaller-engined models now have emissions not much more than 100 grammes per kilometre, while some large executive cars can still sometimes emit 200 grammes or more. The quickest way to take a large slice out of your emissions is to re-equip your fleet with light, small-engined cars. Of course, some people will object to this so you may need to look at other options.

Industry bodies and car leasing companies are at pains to point out that emissions vary substantially between cars that are similar in terms of size and appearance. Very approximately, the lowest emitter in each class of vehicles is about 30 per cent better than the worst-performing vehicle. (Cars are usually divided into nine or more classes. 'Supermini' is one such class, with the lowest-emission supermini emitting less than 100 grammes per kilometre; the highest in the class emits over 140 grammes.)

From the fleet manager's point of view, the important implication is that company car users can be nudged towards lower-emission cars while still giving them access to large or high-status vehicles. In language used elsewhere in this book (see p. 273), decision-makers can 'choice edit' the range of vehicles offered to users, and fleet emissions will fall as a result. The parcel and mail distribution company TNT actively supports this policy: employees eligible for a company car are paid €3,000 over three years for choosing a car with emissions of less than 120 grammes a kilometre. Only very small cars can currently achieve this low level.

Manual transmissions

Cars with automatic transmissions lose more energy during the transfer of the engine's power to the wheels than manual-transmission models. Estimates vary as to the degree of saving, with much depending on how well the car is driven. But most sources suggest that manual cars can obtain about 10 per cent better fuel consumption. Of course, for many users who have to drive in heavy traffic, a manual transmission is far less pleasurable to drive.

Alternative fuels

Switching a car to liquid petroleum gas (LPG) will help reduce emissions, though the savings are quite small and the cost of conversion is not insignificant. In addition, LPG fuel can be hard to find in some areas. 'Dual fuel' cars that can run on conventional petrol and on LPG avoid this problem, but it probably doesn't make financial sense to retrofit a car with dual-fuel capability.

Hybrids

Hybrid electric cars, such as the Toyota Prius, have batteries that are recharged by capturing some of the energy lost when the car brakes. There are three principal benefits of having this supplementary battery. First, the car's engine can be turned off when the vehicle stops temporarily, perhaps at traffic lights. Second, the energy stored in the battery will replace petrol that would otherwise be used. And third, a hybrid's engine can be slightly smaller than it would otherwise be. The importance of the engine size is principally in helping cars accelerate faster;

a hybrid's battery provides a bit of extra push when the accelerator pedal is depressed, meaning the engine can be smaller, thereby reducing fuel consumption.

The Prius offers one of the best-measured fuel economies on the road today. Although a small eco-car such as the VW Polo Blue Motion or the Citroën C1 have similar emissions, they are very much smaller cars. In other words, the Prius is a car deemed appropriate for high-ranking executives, whereas few company bosses are prepared to drive superminis.

Hybrid technology can be used in commercial vehicles as well, though progress has been slow even in urban buses, where the savings are most obvious.

Electric cars and vans

Progress towards fully electric cars is surprisingly fast. Although most people think that battery-only vehicles are slow and ponderous, new electric cars can now offer acceleration and comfort that matches conventional vehicles. They are still expensive – largely because of the batteries – but cost improvement is likely to be rapid. The UK's best-established electric vehicle manufacturer says that more progress has been made in the last year than in any previous year in history, essentially because batteries are getting cheaper and quicker to charge.

Electricity isn't a 'zero-carbon' fuel – it is generated in large power plants, mostly burning coal and gas. An extra kilowatt hour of electricity produced in the UK typically puts another half-kilogramme of CO_2 into the atmosphere. But because an electric car or van converts about 80 per cent of the power in its batteries to motion on the road, it will generally have a fraction of the carbon footprint of a diesel vehicle travelling the same distance.

How suitable are these vehicles for commercial use? Although most people think that electric cars and vans are slow and unreliable, they can be built to accelerate faster than a petrol engine and have top speeds at least as high as conventional equivalents. But hard acceleration does drain a battery quickly, so commercial electric vehicles will often have their speed capped at 50 miles per hour. A range of about 100 miles between charges is fine for runs around crowded cities, but a few trips to the suburbs each day will rapidly empty the battery.

Such limitations will be removed over time by longer-life batteries or the creation of 'refuelling' points where run-down batteries can be quickly removed and replaced with freshly charged equivalents. This is the model being pushed by Shai Agassi, the entrepreneur behind Californian electric car start-up Project Better Place. His business is targeting countries with large resources of renewable energy, such as Denmark with its wind farms and Israel with its plentiful sun for solar power. It remains to be seen if the model will catch on.

In the interim, there's one really obvious market for battery vehicles in business – as delivery vans in crowded cities. Since they generally don't travel long distances, battery life is not a serious problem. They almost all return to the depot every night and they can be easily recharged.

Electric vans and lorries

Smith Electric Vehicles has been making battery-powered commercial vehicles for over 90 years. The company originally focused on smaller runarounds like electric mail vans but it has more recently started to specialise in larger vehicles for trades people – such as the Ampere 2.3-tonne van – and bigger lorries for urban delivery routes.

The initial capital cost of electric vehicles is much higher than traditional vehicles – up to twice as much according to one customer that is trialling electric delivery vans in London. But you can get 100 per cent depreciation in the first year under the Enhanced Capital Allowances scheme (see p. 287). And once you have the vehicle, the running costs are extremely low. Smith suggested a figure for electricity costs as low as 1.2 pence per mile for the Ampere; the diesel equivalent would be over ten times higher than this. In some public car parks in London you can even get free electricity for your battery-powered vehicle.

Electric vans are easier to maintain, too. Smith points out that its vans have only four or five moving parts compared to about a thousand in an internal combustion engine. They only sell their vehicles to companies with larger fleets because they want the vans to be professionally maintained, but the costs should be a fraction of the servicing bills of diesel equivalents. They are also free of road fund tax and are exempt from the London congestion charge.

The manufacturer claims that the total lifetime costs of an electric van are already probably 20–30 per cent lower than a diesel equivalent. This figure includes the depreciation of the vehicle, fuel, maintenance and road taxes. The advantage will be eroded if the price of diesel reverts to cheaper levels. Nevertheless, the long-run downward trend in battery costs means that electric delivery vans will eventually be cheaper than fossil-fuel vehicles.

Several major companies are running trials of electric delivery trucks in the capital. One is Office Depot, the large stationery company that operates the Viking Direct brand. It offers same-day delivery to some parts of London. Office Depot has bought a Smith Electric 3.5-tonne lorry and it provided me with some of the figures from its business appraisal of the case for buying such a vehicle. FedEx is using vehicles from Modec, Smith's main UK competitor. The FedEx vehicles use the same approach as Project Better Place: the batteries can be taken out when empty and fully charged replacements inserted.

Total running costs of the vehicle over a five-year period

Electricity	£2,600
Diesel fuel	£15,500
Difference	£12,900 cheaper for electric lorry
Maintenance for electric lorry	£1,800
Maintenance for diesel lorry	£4,900
Difference	£3,100 cheaper for electric lorry

Office Depot told me that it believed it would also save £10,000 from not having to pay the London Congestion Charge over five years. This turned the balance firmly towards buying electric delivery vehicles for use in the city. So far, the trial is going well.

Besides reducing costs and emissions, electric vans and

lorries also avoid the problems of local air pollution that
come from using even the most efficient diesel vehicles.
And for vehicles that need to deliver to offices, there's also a
small but real advantage because electric vans and trucks
are virtually noiseless. The Mayor of London is actively supporting low-carbon vehicles like these, which help to reduce
noise pollution.

Stop & Start technology

Refinements to combustion-engine technology will be slow
and incremental, and we are never going to see a petrol engine
that is as efficient as an electric car. In fact, the single most productive improvement to engines that we can expect to see
soon is Stop & Start. This technology turns the engine off
when the car comes to a halt and restarts it almost instanta-
neously when the driver signals an intention to move (usually
by depressing the clutch to put the car in gear). The delay is
less than half a second.

The fuel savings of Stop & Start depend primarily on where
the vehicle is being driven. When driving in busy towns, cars
frequently stop and start. A driver will often spend more time
stationary than in motion. At such times, normal cars waste a
lot of petrol just keeping the engine ticking over. Manufacturers like Citroën say that the fuel savings can be up to 15 per
cent in heavy traffic. On longer journeys on main roads, the
saving is less – perhaps just 5 per cent. The savings on diesel
cars are somewhat lower, largely because this type of internal
combustion engine uses less fuel when idling at traffic lights.

Stop & Start technology is likely to become standard fairly soon. At several hundred pounds, the incremental cost is currently quite high, but this will come down sharply when the equipment is installed in millions of cars every year. For drivers doing tens of thousands of miles a year, Stop & Start technology is already very good value – and certainly something worth looking at by fleet managers.

Car clubs

Organisations can sometimes save money and emissions by using car clubs to provide flexible mobility for their employees. The car club – usually a private, profit-making enterprise – provides one or more vehicles to your business premises. These cars can be booked online and used by any employee who needs them. Each employee has a key and can be asked to record the purpose of his or her trip on private pages on the car club's website. The cost can be calculated after the trip and allocated to particular budgets or departments.

An important advantage of providing cars in this way is that it avoids the need to tax employees for the private use of their car. The business also avoids the accounting complexity of paying people for business mileage driven in their own cars. Car club operators also comment that providing pooled vehicles reduces the incentive for several people to travel to the same destination in their own cars, all claiming business mileage. They can also encourage employees to make rational and thought-through decisions about how to get from place to place, and even whether travel is really necessary. The UK best-established car clubs – Streetcar, CityCar

Club and Zipcar – all offer businesses highly automated booking and reporting processes, and cost-competitive new cars.

The core business of car clubs is providing shared cars in residential streets for individuals, not businesses. These businesses say that many people get rid of their own cars when they become members of car clubs and drive far fewer miles each year, sometimes saving thousands of pounds. By one estimate, each club car placed on the street removes at least six other vehicles. So car clubs are convincingly green in residential areas and are almost certainly a good, financially appropriate idea for business as well.

Biofuels – a way of reducing your corporate emissions?

When a plant or tree grows, it extracts carbon dioxide from the atmosphere to build the carbon-based molecules that form its structure. The photosynthesis process takes energy from the sun's light rays and uses it to extract the carbon from atmospheric CO_2, bond it with other atoms and create complex energy-rich hydrocarbon molecules. Similarly, the fruits and seeds of a plant ultimately derive from the carbon in the air, water and soil nutrients. The molecules that provide much of the structure of a tree – usually a mixture of cellulose and lignin – are complex and tough. It uses a lot of energy to break them down, and we don't yet know how to make large quantities of fuel from these large, tough molecules. But most fruits and seeds are composed of relatively simple sugars that can easily be cracked to create a valuable fuel called ethanol –

more colloquially known as alcohol. Ethanol can be added to petrol, and it helps to provide the energy to drive the car. In fact, many cars can be run on 85 per cent ethanol with only a small amount of petrol.

In theory, ethanol is a green fuel because it is derived from plant sources that have previously captured CO_2 from air. When the fuel is burnt, it simply returns an equivalent amount of carbon dioxide to the atmosphere. The CO_2 would have gone back into the air anyway as the plant rotted. Unfortunately, it is not quite as simple as this. Growing crops in temperate regions requires large amounts of energy from fossil-fuel sources. Wheat, the most important native-grown source of ethanol in the UK, needs to be cultivated and heavily fertilised. The application of the fertiliser to the soil produces a small amount of nitrous oxide, a global-warming gas over 300 times as powerful as CO_2. After the wheat is harvested, the processes to turn the grain into a biofuel require large amounts of heat, usually provided from fossil fuels. All in all, the greenhouse-gas savings from using wheat to make ethanol are likely to be quite small, perhaps as little as 30 per cent of the emissions from petrol.

The calculations are better when making ethanol from sugar cane grown in Brazil. However, if we increase the acreage devoted to sugar cane in Brazil, we may be indirectly adding to the pressure on the Amazonian rainforest. If Brazilians grow larger and larger amounts of sugar for making fuel, then the country will need to use other land to satisfy the world's food needs. Although sugar cane is grown in fairly dry areas a long way from the rainforest, increasing sugar cane acreage probably indirectly means more deforestation in the Amazon basin.

Ethanol is made from starchy foods to replace some of our needs for petrol. Similarly, a diesel substitute can be made from oil-bearing seeds, such as tropical palms and rape from temperate regions. Unfortunately, the same issues arise with this type of fuel. Seeds take fossil-fuel energy to grow, fertilise and process into a fuel. Using land for biodiesel increases the pressure on the world's forest lands. An acre removed from growing food will probably result in an acre of forest being cut down elsewhere to grow our crops.

In the past, many governments argued that using foods to make petrol and diesel substitutes was a good idea – a small amount of biodiesel or ethanol is now included as a legal requirement in every litre that is sold in the UK. But the tide of support has turned fast. After a couple of years of enthusiastic support of biofuels, many large UK companies have begin to move away from backing the use of agricultural products as the raw materials for fuels. Many large transport companies have decided to abandon plans to use fuels with a large percentage of biological ingredients. National Express has indicated it will not back biofuels for its coach fleet. Tesco, which uses 50 per cent biodiesel in its distribution fleet, seems to be reversing its early support for biofuels. Although the arguments over the carbon savings from using agriculturally derived fuels are complex and far from settled, using biofuels in a corporate fleet currently looks unacceptable; the public-relations consequences of using agricultural-derived ethanol would be negative. And the continuing furore over the destruction of tropical forests in Asia in order to grow palm oil for biodiesel means that no large company could afford to be associated with its use in UK vehicles.

Nevertheless, organisations should not close their minds to the future use of biofuels. Currently, we are using food to make fuels, but we will eventually be able to use the much more abundant cellulose molecule to make very simple chemical compounds such as ethanol. The obstacle at the moment is that cellulose is a very tough molecule and we haven't yet found easy ways to break it into sugars and then ferment it into ethanol. But the day is rapidly coming when we will be able to turn cellulose-based wood wastes – such as bark and sawdust – into motor fuels at reasonable cost. This is called second-generation biofuel or 'cellulosic' ethanol. Wood wastes often have few alternative uses, and we may be able to make cellulose-based petrol substitutes at acceptable cost. At the moment, though, UK companies are probably wise to shy away from fuelling their fleets with biofuels.

Reducing the status attached to performance cars

In the minds of many business-people, a prestigious company car denotes the status of the user – important people are expected to drive expensive cars. Whether we like this or not, we need to acknowledge the vital role that cars play in showing where people stand in the corporate pecking order. Any crude attempt to reduce the total emissions from the car fleet by obliging employees to choose smaller or cheaper vehicles is likely to fail. It will take decades before the connection between seniority and size of car is broken. But there are a few companies where senior managers are less driven by the need for status. In these businesses, the top people have deliberately reduced the size of their cars to set an example to others. This is something that all senior executives should consider.

Government could encourage this trend by continuing to increase the rates of taxation on larger company cars.

Improved driving

Substantial reductions in vehicle fuel use can be achieved by improving driving practices. Accelerating more carefully, keeping the car properly maintained, pumping up car tyres to the correct pressure: small and easy steps that can each improve fuel consumption by a few percentage points. Taken together, they might improve miles-per-gallon (MPG) figures by 10–15 per cent. This is not as important as switching to electric cars or vans, but is nevertheless a worthwhile saving.

Eco-driving

Bad drivers cost a business money – they use more fuel and, more importantly, they have more accidents. This raises the costs of insurance and adds to the burden of administering a car fleet. By contrast, greener drivers are usually safer drivers. They drive more slowly, accelerate carefully and try to predict problems in the road ahead of them – in addition to saving fuel and carbon emissions.

Basically, a driving pattern that consists of rapid acceleration and braking consumes far more fuel than a car driven smoothly and carefully. Speed is also important – a company car driven at 85 mph uses 25 per cent more fuel than one hugging the 70 mph speed limit. Equally, goods vehicles that are speed-limited to 56 mph on motorways can save significant amounts of diesel.

As organisations become more aware of the high cost of poor driving, some are sending their employees on eco-driving courses. Typically, these businesses insist that every driver involved in an accident spends a day learning how to drive more safely and economically. On these courses, the employees learn how to drive conservatively and cut the risk of accidents. Since business car drivers have a much higher risk of accidents than other vehicle users, this will in time reduce the high car insurance premiums paid by many organisations.

Other green driving tips include avoiding unnecessary loads in the car, removing roof racks when not in use and closing windows when the vehicle is in motion; open windows increase aerodynamic drag and mean that the car has to use more fuel to travel at the same speed.

Maintenance

This is probably worth 3 or 4 per cent on fuel economy. You need to replace old air filters, keep the oil topped up and uncontaminated, and ensure that the car or van is correctly tuned. This means that all vehicles need to be serviced at least as frequently as advised by the manufacturer. Though frequent servicing costs more money and may not actually be financially worthwhile, it will undoubtedly reduce fuel consumption across a fleet. Data is sparse, but under-maintained vehicles may have an increased accident risk because of worn tyres or brakes.

Companies that let their employees drive their own vehicles and claim mileage allowances should accept a responsibility for ensuring that the cars of its employees are properly serviced.

Aside from anything else, it cannot be long before businesses are held responsible for avoidable accidents caused by a driver on company business in a badly maintained car. The sensible organisation should take action now to demand to see the servicing records of all vehicles used on business but not owned by the company.

Inflating tyres correctly

Surveys show that most tyres on UK roads are under-inflated, perhaps by as much as 20 per cent. Such tyres represent a safety risk and should be avoided for that reason alone: they don't hold the road as well as tyres at the correct pressure. In addition, because of increased friction between the tyre and the road they increase fuel use by 2–3 per cent. Clearly, then, companies should ensure that all tyres are regularly checked for pressure.

Some people say that tyres lose their pressure more slowly if they are filled with nitrogen rather than air. Perhaps they are taking too much notice of the fact that Formula One racing tyres are inflated this way. Actually, the evidence that nitrogen leaks more slowly from ordinary tyres is limited or non-existent. And it can cost £5 or more to inflate with nitrogen rather than ordinary air – in addition to using more energy. As such, this makes little sense in normal conditions.

Journey planning

Some estimates suggest that the average vehicle drives in the wrong direction 5 per cent of the time. This is wasteful of money, carbon dioxide and time. As prices have reduced over

Michelin's 'green' tyres

Michelin produces 'green' tyres designed to make a real difference to the amount of petrol a driver uses. These low-rolling-resistance tyres cost about £10 more each than their conventional equivalents. If Michelin's claims are correct about the fuel savings – 3 per cent, in addition to better safely and longevity – then it makes sense for almost all business cars to use the product.

By Michelin's calculations, if all the cars and HGVs in Europe were fitted with its green tyres, this would save 4.5 billion litres of diesel, 1.5 billion litres of petrol and 15 million tonnes of CO_2. See www.michelin.com for more information.

the last few years, it almost certainly now makes financial sense for employers to install satellite navigation (sat-nav) systems in the vehicles of all employees who regularly drive on business.

For those vehicle users not using sat-nav equipment, drivers should carefully print off a set of journey instructions from the Internet before leaving on a car journey. This simple tip can save many a wasted mile.

In addition, employees need to be encouraged to share journeys and to question whether the trip is really necessary. In some companies, it would be a major culture change to insist on employers being asked for a short written justification of any car trip undertaken when the destination is not a customer premises, but it would be a powerful signal of senior management's commitment to reducing the amount of car travel.

Many companies have put considerable effort into minimising the number of miles driven by part-full or empty vehicles. The grocery chains, which are probably directly and indirectly responsible for a quarter of the heavy goods vehicles on Britain's roads, are making measurable reductions in fuel consumption in this way. Combined with slow but real transfers of food and drink shipments to the railway network, the large retailers are gradually reducing unnecessary mileage.

In-vehicle telematics

Today's technology gives organisations the option of installing electronics in vehicles to log speed, acceleration and braking, as well as signalling the vehicle's location; essentially, employers can tell where a vehicle is and how well it is being driven. Drivers who breach speed limits, wrongly use cars for personal mileage or repeatedly waste fuel by rapid acceleration can be identified. Telematics give employers an extra tool to reduce emissions from car and commercial vehicle travel.

Many people will have concerns about the invasion of privacy resulting from the use of vehicle telematics. But some organisations are now almost obliged to use vehicle tracking as a means of ensuring the safety of their mobile employees. The evidence from users suggests that vehicle telematics do reduce the mileage driven and decrease fuel use because vehicles are driven more efficiently. Nevertheless, one large fleet manager told me that the cost of sophisticated equipment, plus the monthly charges from the mobile phone companies that carry the data back to the company every few seconds, meant that it isn't yet economical for most companies to operate telematics systems. This will eventually change, and for many companies a continuous reporting system will help cut down poor driving and unnecessary mileage.

Cutting employee commuter travel

This is tricky. You want your employees to drive less, but you know that many people have to take a car to work. You know that the time will come when you will be expected to declare employee commuting mileage in your corporate social responsibility reports. The problem is, there isn't a decent or reliable public transport alternative for many of your employees.

You can encourage car sharing by incorporating a simple booking scheme on your company intranet. Perhaps you could also offer small financial inducements. An organisation might in addition provide a high-quality shuttle bus service from the main local transport hubs to your offices (Sky does this very successfully in west London). Another tactic that has worked in some companies has been to devote the best places in the company car park to those employees who share cars. At one large company in Swindon, this technique substantially changed behaviour because it meant that car-sharing employees guaranteed that they could find a place in an otherwise very crowded company car park. Barclaycard dedicates 300 places at its Northampton HQ to cars arriving with more than one occupant.

Liftshare is a scheme that enables people to ask for and offer shared journeys. Its website can be used by individual companies to provide a place for employees to check whether other people are making the same journey at the same time. The Liftshare service can also be customised to offer a taxi-sharing service. Look at various case histories about the impact on corporate profits at www.liftshare.com.

Using public transport

Many organisations have made sustained efforts to encourage employees to shift from car to rail travel. How much CO_2 this saves depends not only on the car but also whether the rail journey is on a diesel or an electric line, and whether the train uses heavy modern carriages and power units, or lighter older carriages. Across all types of journeys, however, trains are about three times as efficient as a business car with one person on board.

Rail journeys in comfortable first-class accommodation often seem expensive and time-consuming – peak-time journeys are invariably pricey and the carriages are usually crowded. But, when compared with car travel, the railways are usually good value in terms of pence per mile. Just as importantly, employees can often work productively on the train, particularly if they are equipped with mobile broadband and laptops. Not only will most rail journeys save time, but they can also help by imposing discipline on the length of meetings. If people know they have to catch a particular train, the meeting can be more purposeful and focused.

Removing unproductive incentives to travel by car

One of the most pernicious features of business and public-sector life is the practice of paying people to drive their car. If, like most organisations, you reimburse the cost of driving a private car on company business, you are probably encouraging your employees to use their vehicle at times when it isn't strictly necessary. Offer more than 20 pence reimbursement per mile and most users will be making what they think of as a profit when they use their car. So people are willing to drive when they ought to be thinking about sharing cars or not travelling at all.

One car-leasing company told me of a public-sector organisation that paid its employees an allowance of 50 pence a mile (higher than the rate authorised by the government's taxation body, HMRC). As a result, all staff travel as much as they can by car. The leasing company had spoken to one driver who had boasted that his business mileage had paid for his previous year's holiday. In such a system, three or four people travelling to the same place at the same time will always take their own cars – even when completely unnecessary.

One way of systematically diminishing the incentive to drive is to reduce the price paid per mile so that drivers no longer seen any reason to use their car. It may also make sense to formally discourage car use. Recently, some organisations have been trying to switch employees into company vehicle schemes. The company can sometimes ensure that these people are able to obtain the preferential car prices paid by the business. These are generally about 20 per cent below conventional retail prices. The employee will still own the vehicle, but can be paid lower rates per mile, and will be responsible for less CO_2 when driving. One study suggests that the 'grey fleet', or the cars owned by employees on business trips, has average emissions of about 20 grammes per kilometre higher than the equivalent business-owned car. So encouraging employees to buy new cars from the organisation's recommended list makes good sense.

Greening the car fleet: case studies

TNT policy statement

The distribution company TNT has a thorough plan for reducing emissions from company cars. It is reproduced here as an example of a robust policy statement from a major user of cars and commercial vehicles. Note the incentives given to employees to choose low-emissions vehicles, and the emphasis placed on proper reporting of mileage and on driver training. While the target to cut emissions by 6 per cent by 2011 may not seem appropriately ambitious, it should be remembered that this is in the context of a growing business that would otherwise have seen a substantial increase in fuel use.

1. Policy Objective

As part of TNT's goal to significantly cut its CO_2 emissions, TNT aims to reduce CO_2 emissions from company cars by 6 per cent by 2011 (compared to 2006 levels).

The objectives of this policy are therefore to ensure that:

- all company cars meet increasing fuel efficiency standards.
- employees drive company cars safely and efficiently.
- fuel usage and distance data are accurately recorded and reported.
- employees are encouraged to select very fuel-efficient cars.

2. Policy Statement

From 1 June 2007:

- all new TNT company cars must meet fuel efficiency standards established by TNT.

- all drivers of company cars must complete training for safe and fuel-efficient driving.

- all drivers of company cars must record and report fuel and distance data.

- a one-off incentive payment will be given to all employees who select cars that produce emissions lower than 120 grammes of CO_2 per kilometre.

- a car allowance will not normally be permitted as an alternative to a company car except where it currently exists as part of the terms and conditions of an entity; in such a case, it will continue to apply to both existing and new employees.

- a car allowance must not be introduced into entities where it does not exist at the date this policy is implemented.

3. Implementation

Eligible vehicles

Every time a TNT employee selects a new car, he or she must select a model that meets the fuel efficiency standards established by TNT.

Eligible vehicles are presented on the website. The site will be updated regularly as new models become available.

Local policies will apply on the selection of vehicles and employees must consult with their managers before selecting a vehicle.

Incentive for selecting very fuel-efficient cars

Employees who select very fuel-efficient vehicles (those that produce emissions lower than 120 grammes of CO_2 per kilometre) will receive a one-time gross cash payment of €3,000, paid at the rate of €1,000 per annum over three years and taxable in accordance with local requirements.

The TNT Board of Management will annually review the amount of this incentive and the CO_2 threshold.

Training for safe and fuel-efficient driving

Within six months of receiving a company car, all drivers must attend training on safe and fuel-efficient driving. This training may be provided by the leasing agency or another recognised competent provider.

Fuel usage and distance recording and reporting

All drivers of company cars must provide data about their fuel usage and distances driven on a continual basis. This process may be supported by leasing agencies, which often have onboard computers and at-the-pump data reporting systems in place.

BT's travel policies

BT is widely seen as an environmental leader, and its policies have delivered substantial reductions in emissions. Because of the surging growth of data storage, it faces a difficult challenge to stabilise and reduce its overall emissions. But it has achieved a lot in the field of road travel. The chart and text overleaf are taken from BT's most recent report on sustainability, showing what the company has done in the last year to improve the CO_2 footprint of its cars and vans. Once again, this example is chosen to demonstrate the importance of taking a range of actions to manage vehicle emissions.

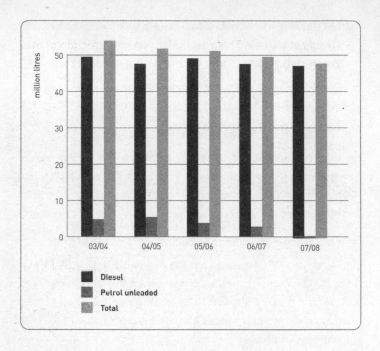

Initiatives undertaken in the 2008 financial year

- Trained 50 engineers in fuel-efficient driving techniques to assess fuel savings and determine our approach to future training.

- 4,299 new vehicles ordered during the 2008 financial year limited to 70 mph (where this is offered by the manufacturer) and labelled with a 'green' message.

- Assessed the market for suitable electric vehicles to trial.

- Conducted a series of fuel trials as part of the selection process for new light and medium vans.

- BT Supply Chain consolidated its deliveries to BT sites so that each site was visited just once a week instead of up to 5 times in a week. This resulted in a fleet reduction of over 70 vehicles.

Reducing CO_2 from business car travel: a summary

Vehicle and fuel choice

Diesel, not petrol	Diesel cars of the same size and power are approximately 15% lower emitters
Manual, not automatic	Not suitable for all drivers, but manual cars typically have 10% better fuel consumption
Choose lowest-emitting car within your preferred class of vehicle	30% gap between best and worst among similar-sized and -powered cars. Important for managers to 'choice edit' the list of cars available for company car users
Smaller cars	Best new cars are now at about 100 g/km, compared to over 200 g/km for a large, inefficient car
Electric cars and vans	Probably a good alternative already for city vans and light trucks. Cost of ownership lower even though capital cost is higher.
Hybrids	Expensive for the emissions reductions that they generate but can help persuade top management to drive low-CO_2 cars.
Stop & Start	Only available on a small number of cars but makes sense for heavy urban drivers

▶

Reducing the status attached to performance cars	Top management needs to set an example
Driving better	
Eco-driving	Accelerate slowly, travel at no more than speed limit, avoid driving that requires frequent harsh braking, keep windows closed, remove excess weight and roof racks
Maintenance	Service car regularly
Tyres	Ensure tyres are at correct pressure to help minimise rolling resistance
'Green' tyres	Reduces rolling resistance
Driving less	
Journey planning	Use sat-nav or plan route by carefully using maps
Cutting employee commuter travel	Incentivise car sharing and use of public transport
Using public transport	Carefully calculate the real costs of driving rather than using trains and, where appropriate, encourage the use of rail
Removing unproductive incentives to travel by car	Ensure reimbursement arrangements do not encourage excessive car travel
Avoiding the need to travel	Better planning and allocation of work tasks and use of Internet collaboration tools such as video-conferencing

Air travel

After electricity use, business air travel is often the second largest source of emissions by large companies. Some smaller companies engage in large amounts of air travel, too, though in most cases car emissions are a bigger issue for them.

The most efficient modern planes now operate with CO_2 output that is better per passenger, per mile, than a typical car being driven solo. However, this does not make air travel a good method of travel, environmentally speaking. For one thing, aircraft produce pollutants other than carbon dioxide. The effect of these pollutants is not well understood by scientists and further work will be required before the effect can be quantified accurately, but the evidence is that the emissions of water vapour, nitrous oxide and other pollutants may double or triple the effect of the carbon dioxide alone.

The second point is that air travel involves very long distances. The distance travelled by the average British car in a year is less than a single flight to Los Angeles and back. Some senior executives will make many air journeys of this length each year. Large international companies function by involving their people in a continuous criss-crossing of people from office to office.

The UK is particularly reliant on air travel – about 6 per cent of UK CO_2 emissions come from civil aviation, and this number is rising as leisure and business travel expands. (But at the time of writing it looks possible that 2008 actually may see a reduction in fuel used because of the high price of oil and declining economic growth.) If we apply the multiplier of three to reflect the impact of other pollutants, the figure becomes more than a tenth of total UK greenhouse gases. Respected academic researchers such as Alice Bows at the Tyndall Centre rightly suggest that if the country as a whole needs to cut its emissions to 20 per cent of recent levels, aviation – which is still growing rapidly – will quickly use up all the UK's prospective allowance.

The aviation industry points out that it is improving its record – improved engines and more aerodynamic designs mean that fuel use is falling per kilometre travelled. And, until recently, aircraft were operating at higher capacities, meaning that more people shared the emissions. But in a recession, this trend will probably reverse.

Airlines are also beginning to experiment with renewable jet fuels. Air New Zealand is looking at extracting oil from the berries of the tropical shrub jatropha. This may mean eventually we will not need to use kerosene made from crude oil. But although the use of biofuels may seem to avoid the issue of carbon-dioxide emissions (since the plant extracted CO_2 from the air when growing), it does nothing to reduce the emissions of the other pollutants, which are at least as important. Moreover, it seems likely that jatropha berries will grow best on arable lands, reducing the amount of food available for the world's population. We cannot totally dismiss the value of next-generation bio-kerosene, but we face huge challenges making it from a sustainable source that doesn't impact the world's availability of food and other products of the land, such as wood for use in cooking stoves.

In my view, it is at least possible that companies and governments will face increasing societal pressures to fly less within the next few years. These pressures may take the form of higher taxes, tighter emissions caps or other restrictions. Organisations that encourage flying – particularly of the small private jets that are particularly heavy users of fuel per passenger mile – may face damage to their brand image. A corporate away-day in Malaga is not entirely consistent with a marketing push that tries to represent the organisation as ethically responsible. Of course, unnecessary travel will also be seen as financially irresponsible in a recession.

So what can be done?

- Some corporate travel is not necessary. Following this section, I look at online collaboration and at video-conferencing. Both can reduce the need for flights.

- Perhaps more importantly, many organisations can reduce air travel by enforcing policies that demand reasonable justification for trips. All of us hear stories of leisure trips disguised as business travel, attendance at unnecessary meetings on the other side of the world and ill-disciplined management that creates the need for excessive flying.

- Large amounts of travel within the UK and western Europe are at least as quick by train. Most people also describe the experience as more pleasant than flying.

- If travel has to take place, it makes sense to use airlines that have modern, efficient jets that are usually full. The emissions from a flight on a low-cost airline are generally going to be substantially lower than the equivalent trip on a national carrier.

These recommendations are all very well, but most organisations are still reporting rising volumes of business travel among their employees. Economic recession will temporarily reverse this trend, but looking at the published environmental reports of our largest companies, air travel is proving hard to control. Organisations may therefore want to invest in offsetting (see p. 261) to minimise the impact of their travel. Offsetting has its critics, but I think that purchasing emissions permits from the European Emissions Trading Scheme is as good a system as any for reducing the environmental impact of aviation. This idea is covered in more detail on p. 271.

Reducing the need for travel

The face-to-face meeting is an important part of business, since getting to know someone personally helps build commercial relationships. Just as an organisation wouldn't dream of recruiting someone without interviewing them in person, businesses accept that their staff members need to meet customers and suppliers face-to-face. Similarly, at least in theory, meetings between colleagues help them develop trust and productive business friendships. There is no easy substitute for meetings – they perform a function that sometimes cannot be replicated by telephone calls or even the latest video-conferencing tools. Meetings also help people sense what is really going on inside an organisation, as opposed to what the press releases say. Most companies, particularly large ones, have diffuse and unclear structures of authority and communication. The body language of the boss at the end of the table often says more than a thousand emails.

But much corporate travel is unnecessary, and very expensive in time, money and carbon emissions (see box below). Is that get-together in Cologne really necessary? Do you actually need a half-day conference in Birmingham to share the latest research results? Advances in low-cost telecommunications tools make it possible to reduce corporate travel by a surprisingly high amount. Some estimates say 20 per cent, others go as high as a half.

The true cost of business travel

www.flexibility.co.uk, the online journal of flexible working, stresses that the cost of travel doesn't end with the price of the plane or train ticket. Here's their advice, reproduced by kind permission:

Changing the way people work is no small undertaking. And it will require some investment to make the savings. The evidence base must be substantial. So for this reason it is important to build up a picture of the **total travel costs**.

These consist of:

- **direct travel expenses** – petrol, mileage, tickets, meals, accommodation, etc.: ie everything usually counted under travel expenses
- **time costs** – the salary costs of people while they are being unproductive or less productive in transit
- **travel investment** – eg in company car fleets, leasing arrangements, parking spaces, etc.
- **travel administration** – time spent in organising travel, processing and reimbursing expenses, etc.

▶

Take for example four people coming to a two-hour meeting, each travelling for an hour each way. Eight hours' travel, a day's worth of productivity, has gone into just travelling for the meeting. But more than that, additional direct and indirect administrative time has gone into it. The results may be worth it. But how many people coming away from a meeting would say that it is true in most cases?

And the two hours of the meeting. Are they truly justified as the time needed for doing the business? Rarely so. The value of this time is hard to quantify: but what is the cost of the 'padding' of the meeting – the sharing of information that could more easily have been sent ahead online, not to mention the posturing and the waffle and digressions.

It's important to look on travel in a neutral way, however, and not to demonise it. Business travel is associated with many positives for the business – meeting clients, solving their problems, selling things to them, developing new partnerships, managing effectively across sites, and so forth. The question is not 'Should we do it?', but rather, 'Are we doing much more of this than we need to?'

In addition, many employees think that they have to attend too many meetings. They resent both the time spent on travel and the loss of normal productivity during their absence from the office. Family life is disrupted and employee motivation is reduced. The amount of travel getting to these meetings is increasing. More than nine million people passed through Heathrow in 2005 on the way to internal company events, almost as many as those visiting customers. This number was up half a million on five years before. Increases in global trade and in corporate mergers of companies on different continents are also tending to increase the distance travelled to such meetings.

Do these meetings have to be face-to-face? BT recently presented some data on the success of its internal voice conferencing system. It said that more than two million telephone conferences took place inside the company. BT estimates a saving of over £200m from the use of this technology and a reduction of almost 100,000 tonnes of CO_2. Typically, these multi-person phone conferences each avoided travel of several hundred miles. BT also said that use of voice conferencing at Tesco, one of its customers, improved an office worker's productivity by 18 per cent. Each phone meeting saved an average of almost £200 in travel costs.

Of course, BT has a clear interest in advocating phone meetings. It is, after all, a telecommunications company. But the figures are very impressive none the less, and not just in terms of carbon savings: the cost reductions are at least as eye-catching. Indeed, switching to video- and audio-conferencing has important implications for profitability. The latest technologies for improving online collaboration are discussed below.

How did businesses manage before business travel?

When researching the early history of the **Oxford English Dictionary**, Professor Charlotte Brewer was struck by the differences in working styles before the arrival of easy travel, ▶

computers or even widespread availability of telephones.
How did the employees working on this great project co-
operate together? One editor was in Chicago, one in
Aberdeen and other important individuals worked away from
Oxford. Surprisingly, perhaps, she found what now seems an
almost astonishing reliance on short, pithy office memos.
Huge numbers of simple and unambiguous written messages moved between the various individuals working on the
dictionary. Meetings were infrequent but were properly
minuted with clear actions demanded of attendees. Although
telephones were available for senior staff, they seem to have
been rarely used.

Perhaps most surprisingly to today's generation of business
managers, people working in nearby offices in the same
building wrote as many memos to each other as they did to
remote colleagues. The carefully written memo (even the
word now sounds dated) can replace an hour's rambling and
an inconclusive discussion. The communications that
Charlotte Brewer studied were almost always simple and
responses terse and quick. A typical written note elicited a
short reply scrawled on the original memo. Though emails
are a key tool, other modern communications techniques –
with their avoidance of direct instruction from manager to
subordinate and frequent use of corporate cliché, vogue
words and euphemistic obfuscation – help make frequent
meetings and long travel necessary. It runs strongly against
the current corporate culture, but a 'green' organisation may
well need to be more directive and hierarchical, with clearer
chains of internal command and a culture more like a mili-
tary organisation than the loose confederations we see today.

Online tools to reduce the need for business travel

Let's look at the hierarchy of ways of using telecommunications to reduce corporate travel:

- Email
- Telephone discussions
- Teleconference with more than two participants
- Teleconference with webcams
- Shared computer screens alongside audio-conferencing
- Full-scale online collaboration, perhaps with small-screen video-conferencing
- Low-bandwidth computer-to-computer video-conferencing
- Full-room video-conferencing.

Email

Email conversations between colleagues or between staff members and customers or suppliers are usually informal, unfocused and extemporary. There's nothing wrong with this, but they tend to complement meetings, rather than replace them. Few email interactions seem to result in real decisions or clear plans of action. Indeed, the informal and often imprecise language of emails can impede the transmission of information and instructions. This may simply be a feature of modern business culture, which prizes freshness and instantaneous response, but it inevitably tends to increase the need for face-to-face meetings.

Telephone discussions

Some telephone calls can avoid the need for a meeting. A well-structured and planned call will enable the participants to sort out a plan of action, reach a decision or communicate information. But in many cases a phone conversation simply lays the ground for a future meeting that will often formalise a decision that could actually have taken place over the phone. A green organisation will try to make telephone conversations more structured and more oriented towards making productive steps forward.

Teleconferencing

Telephone calls between multiple persons are now cheap and extremely simple to organise. Users call in to a number and can hear and speak to all the other persons in the conference call. Commercial providers of this service now often offer it for 'free' – conference participants will pay for the cost of the call and nothing else. Some commercial operators use 'national rate' numbers, costing the user perhaps 8 pence a minute from a landline. The provider makes its money from taking a percentage of the phone charges. You can see how this sort of service works at websites such as www.powwownow.co.uk or www.conferencenow.co.uk.

The major advantage of a telephone conference is that it is usually carefully planned in advance: the instigator decides whom to invite and who is to 'chair' the meeting, a time is precisely set and some form of agenda is usually provided. People receive advance notification of what is to be discussed. This makes it much more likely that they will prepare properly. And if people don't sign in on time, teleconferences usually go ahead without the participant. This makes participants more likely to make the effort to call in to the conference on time.

All these aspects of a telephone conference can make them more productive than a conventional face-to-face meeting, as well as saving money and greenhouse-gas emissions if the participants would otherwise have had to travel.

Teleconferencing with webcams

Any modern computer – desktop or laptop – can provide basic video-conferencing tools. All you need is a broadband connection, an inexpensive webcam (which many laptops and some desktops have built-in) and some software. You can get free person-to-person video-conferencing via providers such as Skype (www.skype.com) or many other commercial companies, as well as all the main instant-messaging services such as Windows Messenger. The video quality on many of these services is poor and the latency (time-lag) can be annoying. They will tend to work best when the people on the call are well known to each other. If you are a friend or a long-term colleague, you can 'see through' the poor-quality video and communicate normally with the other person. But if you barely know the individual, the slowness, poor video quality and mismatch between audio and video can be counter-productive (see box overleaf).

Shared computer screens alongside audio-conferencing

Since video-conferencing doesn't always work as desired, particularly between people who don't know each other well, it

What goes wrong with video-conferencing?

Video-conferencing can be great, but it can also be awful – especially with low-end technology. Here are some of the potential problems:

- Audio needs to be synched with video, but sound is easier to process and tends to arrive first. If the voice reaches the listener too early, the speaker tends to be perceived as untrustworthy and glib. If an adjustment is made to correct this and the video arrives first, the remote person can be seen as being slow-to-understand.

- Social protocols demand that people look at each other directly. A conferencing system that gives the user an impression that his or her interlocutor is looking more than 3 degrees away from the eyes will make the user uncomfortable, and give an impression of disrespect.

- Successful oral communication demands rapid and seamless switching between people in the conversation. Bad video-conferencing makes this more difficult than in an audio call.

- Most clues to the speaker that he or she is boring the audience, confusing them or patronising them are non-verbal. For example, few people actually say that a conversation bores them; they give subtle and not so subtle clues to their conversation partner. Video-conferencing prompts the bored person to offer these clues, but they are sometimes received slowly or not at all by the other person. The speaker does not adjust his or her communication style, and irritation ensues.

- Similarly, people implicitly expect video-conferencing

technologies to make their speech persuasive (which is one of the reasons why one wants to speak face-to-face). It can have the opposite effect.

In summary, bad video is worse than no video. The availability of a picture sets up an expectation that normal free-flowing conversation is going to take place, but if the technology isn't working, then the result will be worse than a phone conversation.

can often make more sense to stick with audio-conferencing. If there are documents or a presentation to discuss, either circulate these in advance or consider trying a screen-sharing system, whereby participants can see each other's computer screens. This can be great for collaborating on documents – from copywriting through to spreadsheets and accounting returns.

Full-scale online collaboration, perhaps with small-screen video-conferencing

The Cisco subsidiary WebEx provides full online collaboration tools that allow presentations and discussions between many individuals. Participants can work with documents, including being able to mark up presentations or spreadsheets. Webcams attached to computers allow the participants to see each other, though this is not generally a central part of online collaboration tools of this sort.

WebEx can be used on a monthly subscription or can be purchased on a per-minute basis. As of the time of writing, this cost is 19p per minute per conference attendee. There's no extra hardware or software to buy. The product also offers high levels of security. See www.webex.co.uk for more information.

Low-bandwidth computer-to-computer video-conferencing

In some circumstances, video 'meetings' are thought to be necessary – people want to see each other, or perhaps discuss how a new product actually looks. As discussed below, some organisations now have sophisticated conference suites that make this possible. However, these systems are extremely expensive to install and to run. They need huge amounts of Internet or private network bandwidth, and very few businesses have more than a handful of locations with such facilities installed.

In many cases, it may make sense to use cheaper but secure video-conferencing that doesn't deliver quite the same quality as the latest 'telepresence' suites but avoids the most severe problems identified in the box on page 206.

The Californian company VSee (www.vsee.com) makes such a product. VSee's system is based on the idea that we don't need high frame-rates to offer real improvements to online video. Cisco provides 30 frames per second, but VSee claims that just 5 are perfectly satisfactory, provided the synch between audio and video is good. Similarly, VSee argues that we don't need a life-size image to talk to, but we do need to offer the ability to look straight into the eye. VSee's system reduces the need for high bandwidth (regular broadband is sufficient), and incorporates various collaboration tools – such as 'laser pens' for PowerPoint presentations – that enable more immediate and compelling mutual understanding. For close collaborators who know each other well, this kind of system is worth exploring.

Full-room video-conferencing

At the very top of the range of collaboration tools, several providers now offer full-room video-conferencing. Despite the fact that AT+T ran the first video-conference right back in 1927, only systems launched recently offer a real alternative to face-to-face meetings.

The telepresence system by Cisco (www.cisco.com/web/UK/solutions) has been on the market for a couple of years, and most users speak glowingly of its usefulness. Other products such as those from Teliris (www.teliris.com) and LifeSize (www.lifesize.com) have also garnered enthusiastic reviews.

What are the key features of these products?

- Video-conferencing takes place in a specially designed room. Each room around the world looks the same, even down to the wallpaper and light fittings. Each 'side' of a video-conference has half an oval table – the other half is in the remote room.

- High-definition LCD screens fill the opposite wall on which clear, life-size images of the people in the other room are shown.

- Video and audio are precisely synched. People look directly at each other and the sound of speech comes from the direction of the other person. One set of user comments suggests that the Teliris product is better than the Cisco version because it gives equal visual 'weight' to people across the remote room, while Cisco's emphasises the centre of the screen.

- Video frame refresh rates are extremely high – 30 new frames a second in some Cisco systems.
- Cisco's product works over the corporation's existing data network (powered by Cisco routers, of course). Teliris offers users its own data network.

The costs are intimidating. To prepare a full room, with several plasma screens on the remote wall, Cisco charges $300,000 (and the same for the other end). A far more restricted product with just one screen sells for $80,000. The monthly cost is said to be '$3–5,000'.

Teliris has recently launched a new set of features that allow users to interact by sharing and editing content on virtual flipcharts. The company claims that people in their telepresence rooms using this new product can benefit from 'gesture recognition algorithms' that allow even more intuitive interactions.

What is going to happen to the costs in the future? Cisco claims that good telepresence products will eventually become viable in the home office. (CEO John Chambers already has one at home.) Others say that the cost will never fall below $10,000 a room. At this level, it may not make sense for many home-workers, but for a senior executive it seems perfectly possible that he or she will eventually equip their office with telepresence equipment that can be linked to hundreds of other offices in the company.

Telepresence in practice

One large international bank I spoke to said that the telepresence room was in high demand, and much liked by those
who used it. The bank was seeing interest from people who
didn't really need the video element of the conversation, and
was restricting its use to the most senior executives only. A
board meeting had taken place via telepresence with one senior
member calling in from London, thus avoiding a long interna
tional flight. These signs look good – if the top people want to
stop the middle ranks from using the rooms, there is clearly a
high status attached to making a video call. If a board meeting
can take place in the rooms, we can see this as a further
endorsement of its acceptability for important discussions.

Other anecdotal material suggests that exposing junior team
members to each other via telepresence has had a good
effect on trust and morale. Many international collaborations
run into the sand because team members do not trust the
other parties to deliver on what they promised. The possibility of holding every participant to account via a telepresence
conversation seems to be improving productivity and providing a sense that people are genuinely working together.

The important point about these technologies – from the
simplest to the most expensive –is not only that they avoid
expensive and time-consuming travel but also that they offer
an opportunity for collaborative working that can be more
productive than conventional business arrangements. Travelling to long meetings that have been poorly planned and
which are then chaired ineptly is costly, demotivating and
may have a large carbon footprint. Modern telecommunications offer the opportunity to build a more effective organisation as well as a greener one.

Teleworking/working from home/ working from anywhere

Increasing numbers of employers are allowing staff to work from home or from some other location that means that they don't have to travel to work as frequently. This saves travel time, fuel and office space, and it seems to make many types of employee more satisfied and productive. (Of course, this cannot be a universal conclusion: a small minority of people are natural shirkers and will achieve much less given the opportunity to be away from the office.)

How about the impact on emissions? That depends on how far your employees commute – and by what means of transport. But even if the distances are small, the savings from reducing office energy use can be considerable. The typical employee in a modern office uses about 5,000 kWh of electricity a year. At home, where no air-conditioning is required, lighting needs are limited and only a certain amount of computing and telecommunications equipment is required, the electricity use per employee is likely to be no more than 1,000 kWh a year.

These savings may be reduced in the winter – especially if your employees heat a large house just to be warm in the room where they're working. And, of course, the energy equation may flip around if many of your staff are working at home but you're simply maintaining – and air-conditioning – a large office full of empty chairs. But there's no doubt that, managed properly, remote working patterns can help reduce emissions.

Several consulting and software companies offer specialised help in getting employees out of centralised offices. PCNow,

The Co-operative Travel – running a contact centre using home-workers

Future Travel is the home-working division of The Co-operative Travel, part of the Co-op group. Future Travel has several hundred part- and full time home-working, self employed advisers, forming the largest home-based service organisation in Europe. The company feeds enquiries out to the staff through a sophisticated call-management system. The agents take about half of the commission they earn, with the company providing substantial back-up. People are properly trained and managed, given access to online travel booking systems and even, in some cases, allowed to package their own holiday deals. Customers benefit from standard UK holiday travel protection and the security of knowing that the agent is backed by the Co-op.

Employee testimonials on the company's website point to the appeal of the independent home-worker model to some types of people. It is clearly valuable to mothers of young children, but also to entrepreneurial and hard-working types who value the opportunity to manage their own activities. And because the work is essentially a sales task, remuneration is clearly tied to an individual's hard work and commitment. There are fewer management problems than there might be with some types of home-working, but the same model could none the less be extended to many other areas.

The green advantages include hugely reduced travel distances, much lower energy consumption and much lower office accommodation costs.

for example, is a product that allows an employee to access their work computer from any location. This software allows the user to work from his or her computer exactly as though they were in the office staring at their usual screen. See www.pcnow.webex.com for more information. 'Thin-client' systems also allow easy remote working and access to corporate data.

Green businesses have made inroads into the volume of supplies they consume.

7

Reducing, reusing and recycling

Office paper, consumables, water and furniture

One of the themes of this book is that productive and success-ful organisations are often those that are most efficient in how they use their resources. Nowhere is this more obviously true than when considering the use of paper and other consum-ables. A tightly managed organisation doesn't need a lot of paper: its business processes are lean and almost everything is done electronically. Resource use can also be minimised by reducing water use and implementing a purchasing policy that gives priority to environmentally friendly office products (something also useful in terms of staff engagement). This chapter looks at each of these issues in turn.

Waste and recycling: the basics

It is better not to produce waste in the first place than to recycle it. Nevertheless, all businesses are going to produce some waste – from catering plastics, cans and food through to electronic items and furniture.

Office paper is by far the most important source of waste for most businesses. As discussed below, it's an environmental no-brainer to recycle it – and an ever-greater proportion of busi-nesses are doing just this. As for other waste streams, most clean plastics, such as water cups, can be easily recycled. It will usually be better to separate the items into different types of plastic – polythene, PET, or polypropylene, for example. Cans, whether steel or aluminium, can also be collected and recycled by specialist firms. Some business recycling services collect for free, and others charge, so be sure to shop around.

There's certainly a lot of room for improvement in the UK. Although around three-quarters of all office waste is recyclable, less than a tenth is actually properly reused. But top-performing companies such as Co-operative Financial Services manage to recycle over 70 per cent of their office waste, and others have made a decision to avoid all waste going to landfill. Even food waste from catering establishments can be composted, or broken in an anaerobic digester; Marks & Spencer has announced plans to use this technology extensively.

When it comes to unwanted furniture, you could try local community enterprises or second-hand shops. Alternatively, use an online donation service such as www.recycle.co.uk or www.freecycle.org. These allow you to offer unwanted items to many thousands of likely takers in one fell swoop. Many 'freecycled' items get collected and removed within a day.

Computer equipment may be worth donating, too. Websites such as www.donateapc.org.uk let you offer PCs, printers and so on to UK-based charities, while others such as www.computeraid.org refurbish computers and make them available for use in the developing world. For more information, explore the directory of services under the computer section of www.wasteonline.org.uk.

The same website also provides a wealth of information on all aspects of waste and recycling – including advice on disposing of metals, fluorescent light bulbs and other items in an environmentally friendly way.

Paper

The use of paper in offices remains stubbornly high. The data is poor, but most estimates suggest that the average office worker in the UK uses about 40 pages of paper a day. Over the year, this amounts to about 17 reams of 500 sheets each; a ream weighs about 2.5 kg.

Many companies use much more. Those businesses that communicate via direct mail, or which have to send out large volumes of paper to customers, find that their paper requirements can be as much as 200 kg per employee. The figure for Aviva, the worldwide insurance company that included the recently re-named Norwich Union among its subsidiaries, is even higher. As a part-time member of the government's Competition Commission, I would sometimes work on cases for which the paperwork would be three or four metres high – or over 150 kg delivered to my office in the space of a few weeks. (Now the Commission does much more on screen and doesn't insist on every document being sent in printed form.)

How important is paper use in terms of a company's carbon footprint? It is far less significant than electricity or travel, but office paper consumption seems to typically represent at least 3–5 per cent of total greenhouse-gas emissions – and far more in companies that produce numerous catalogues or send a lot of direct mail. This is partly because of the large volumes of paper used in most offices, but also because making paper and shipping it long distances is highly energy-intensive. One estimate is that even in the most up-to-date mill a tonne of paper takes about 7,000 kilowatt hours to make. So the average daily consumption of about 40 sheets implies one and a half

Does saving paper save trees?

Buying more paper increases the pollution from paper mills and raises energy use and water consumption. But despite what people might tell you, it will not reduce the size of Europe's forests. Almost all the timber for virgin paper comes from managed forests – for every tree that is cut down, more than one is planted. If anything, increased paper use increases the size of European forests because it increases the incentive to use land to grow trees.

Do we need to use trees at all for paper? What about eco-friendly alternatives such as hemp? It's true that the environmental consequences of using hemp to make paper can be benign compared to using wood, but it's worth bearing in mind that hemp plants compete for land area with food, whereas trees can grow on land that is otherwise largely unusable, such as the northernmost parts of Europe.

kilowatt hours of power consumption a day just in the paper's manufacture. That's close to a tenth of the electricity consumed directly by a UK worker in a modern, energy-intensive office, and the best part of a kilogramme of CO_2 emissions every day.

Some of the UK's paper is made in Scandinavia, where much of the electricity is produced by hydro-electric power plants that create no greenhouse-gas emissions. But if the paper you buy each year is made in the UK in a mill using grid electricity, this would imply a footprint of about 100 kilogrammes of CO_2 per person per year.

Reducing paper use

Most businesses do not maintain accurate figures for their paper consumption. Or, in some cases, the numbers vary so much from year to year that the data is hard to analyse. Three organisations providing robust estimates are shown in the table below.

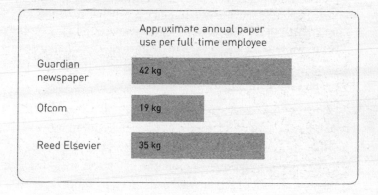

	Approximate annual paper use per full-time employee
Guardian newspaper	42 kg
Ofcom	19 kg
Reed Elsevier	35 kg

Many businesses make some effort to reduce their office paper consumption. We now all get emails that exhort the recipient not to print the message. Unfortunately, the length of these instructions often means that if the recipient disobeys the injunction the email will cover two printed pages rather than one. So the net effect of the message may be small. Other well-tried tactics to reduce paper use include the following:

- Double-sided printing. Although the first office printer that could print on both sides dates from as long ago as 1971, most offices still only use one side of the paper. It makes obvious sense to buy printers that can print on both sides, whether automatically or by requiring the user to manually remove the paper and reload it for the second pass.

- Encouraging employees to print two pages of text on each side of the paper. This can be specified in the 'print option' dialogue box in most applications. However, printing this way will mean that people with poorer eyesight may have problems reading the material.

- Cutting the number of waste-paper bins at desks. Some organisations have got rid of them entirely. Obliging employees to walk to recycling bins to dispose of waste paper seems to have a salutary effect on the amount of material that is printed in the first place.

- Changing the paper stock. The UK uses office paper with a standard weight of 80 grammes per square metre (g/m2). Other countries, including Japan and the US, often use lighter paper weighing no more than 70 g/m2, meaning that the total weight of paper used is reduced by more than 10 per cent. To UK users, this paper can seem insubstantial and flimsy, but it also uses a lot less electricity to make. In fact, the reduction is greater than the percentage reduction in the weight. Similarly, 70 g/m2 requires about a quarter less wood fibre than standard-gauge UK paper. So there is good reason to consider switching.

- Cutting down on paperwork. Some businesses still communicate with regular customers using paper. One major company I have worked for still sends thousands of pages of paper invoices to its largest customer every month. These sheets of paper are then processed by dozens of clerical workers who manually allocate the costs detailed on the invoices to specific projects. In this case, the continued use of paper demonstrates the extraordinary inefficiency of the clerical processes. It would be better both for customer and supplier to work together to ensure that cost centre codes are allocated to the purchase when it is made. Today, almost every piece of paper that flows between two businesses symbolises an inefficiency in business processes. Getting rid of paper is not just green, it also helps simplify operations and makes errors far less likely. Most of the largest companies now use sophisticated document-management software that reduces the need to produce and store paper. Simple versions of this software are available for smaller companies.

- Printing less. Many people absorb information better when the material is presented on paper rather than on a screen. Comparing and annotating documents is also easier if we have printed pieces of paper in front of us. With all that in mind, it seems dangerous for organisations to try to move too aggressively to reduce paper use. But electronic readers (see box overleaf) are getting better every year and it may be possible to eventually adjust conventional working patterns to avoid much of today's paper use.

Recycled paper and paper recycling

There are various reasons why it's environmentally beneficial to use recycled paper whenever possible – and indeed to recycle any paper you need to dispose of. First of all, recycled paper uses far less energy to make. Although the arguments persist, almost all studies show that there are substantial energy savings from taking existing office paper and then recycling it rather than making it from virgin fibre. The savings are certainly more than 3,000 kilowatt hours per tonne

E-readers: will they replace much paper in business?

E-readers – electronic devices for displaying, storing and annotating documents – have been around for several years. Material is loaded on to the reader and the user can then read the text almost as though it is a book. Early e-readers were commercial failures – the text was difficult to read and only a limited range of books were available. But the arrival of Amazon's Kindle began to change this. Kindle can be loaded with documents via a wireless Internet connection. Its screen is highly readable – even in bright sunlight – and it has a large storage capacity – a full novel can be downloaded via US wireless networks in less than a minute.

Evolution of these devices is likely to be rapid. A new version of Kindle is on the way and will work on standard European mobile-phone networks. But this is only the beginning. Cambridge-based Plastic Logic has a truly revolutionary device that may become a close substitute for conventional paper documents – it looks like a thin pad of paper, is extremely robust and can be flexed without damage. It uses the same highly readable e-ink type that makes the Kindle so easy to read. Users can add notes to any material on the screen.

The marketing head at Plastic Logic puts the proposition very clearly: 'The average person only reads two or three books a year, but the same person probably reads several thousand pages of Word, Excel and PowerPoint files at work.' Plastic Logic hopes to replace paper for the executive who has grown tired of shifting large numbers of business documents on trips around the world.

of paper. This means that recycled paper only uses about half as much energy as new paper made from trees.

Recycling also uses far less water than virgin paper. The savings may be as much as 30,000 litres per tonne of paper, which works out at around a sixth of a litre for each piece of A4. (A heavy paper user may consume more water at work through his or her consumption of paper than all other uses combined.) In addition, recycling paper creates much less chemical pollution that making it from scratch.

The price of recycled paper varies, depending on market conditions from day to day. Although it can seem expensive at times, at the time of writing major online retailers were actually selling recycled (standard office) paper at a lower price than the virgin equivalent. And its quality is good; gone are the days when recycled paper was grey and prone to sticking in the photocopier. So there are no business reasons for not using paper that is recycled and making every effort then to ensure that this paper eventually gets back to a paper mill that reuses it. Unfortunately coated papers, such as those often used for direct mail communications with customers, are much more expensive bought in recycled form than as virgin paper.

Paper can be recycled about five times before the fibres become too short to be used again, so a business can put recycled paper back into the loop and the paper can be cleaned, remanufactured and reused. Recycling companies are likely to want you to separate lightly printed white paper (which is more valuable) from coloured papers and documents with lots of printing on them. This means that you will need at least two recycling boxes at each collection point.

Other stationery, office products and equipment

Many businesses are profligate users of other types of office stationery. Controls on what is bought are often poor or non-existent. This is bad for the organisation's carbon footprint. Although office paper is likely to be the most important purchase by most businesses, other products are also worth considering. Responsible businesses need to examine their purchasing policy across all forms of stationery as well as electronic equipment including furniture, computers and photocopiers.

One leading office-products supplier gives its items up to four different labels denoting their green qualities: recycled content, care for woods and forests, environmental benefits compared to conventional alternatives, and supplier commitments to environmental management. This list pretty well sums up the issues, so let's briefly address each point in turn.

Recycled content

Many of the thousands of office stationery products can be bought in recycled form. You can get recycled desk organisers and pens as well as envelopes and other paper stationery. Even if these have minimal measurable benefit on a business's carbon footprint, they may help with staff engagement in green issues. However, these items will usually be substantially more expensive when bought in recycled form.

It depends partly on how the office works, but after paper the most important purchase of recycled goods may be the toner cartridges for laser printers. One source suggests that over four million laser cartridges are dumped every year in the UK.

Many businesses will take your old toner cartridges, renovate them and then refill the product. This can provide both cheaper printing and reduce the numbers of cartridges going to landfill. As with recycled paper, cartridges cannot be economically recycled for ever, but a business that sets up a loop with its suppliers will generally get better value from its toner purchases.

Though it isn't common yet, PCs and photocopiers can also be remanufactured. However, the most important issue when shopping for computers and other electronic equipment isn't recycled components but energy consumption (see p. 92).

Care for woods and forests

Many items purchased by offices are made from wood – not just paper but furniture and much more besides. An environmentally conscious organisation seeks out wood-based items that bear the certification of one of the several bodies that seek to improve the management of forests. The best-known and most widely respected of these is the Forest Stewardship Council (www.fsc.org), an international association that promotes and monitors responsible, long-sighted management of forests. The FSC logo on a book or a pad of paper is meaningful, so be prepared to pay a bit extra.

Be particularly careful buying furniture: it sometimes uses unsustainably harvested wood, and is also expensive to replace. Will your decision to refit offices using hardwoods from an unknown source look appropriate in five years' time? Or should you be spending 20 per cent more in order to get office tables that both look good and won't embarrass the company at some point in the future?

Environmental benefits compared to conventional alternatives

Many stationery products and manufactured goods can be made in several different ways. Some are environmentally neutral with few consequences for ecosystems, others are deeply damaging. These poor manufacturing techniques use large amounts of water, involve nasty chemical processes that result in dangerous discharges into streams and rivers that leave toxic residues. Green-minded organisations need to ruthlessly exclude the goods that damage the environment most. Almost no manufacturing process is truly harmless, but the sensible company looks five years ahead and seeks to focus its purchasing (as well as its own manufacturing processes, of course) on goods and services that are likely to hold their value in an ever more environmentally conscious world.

Supplier commitments to environmental management

Ten years ago, you might have bought your main stationery items based on price, durability and appearance. Today, if you are an environmental leader, your criteria will sensibly include the impact of manufacturing processes on local pollution, whether the raw materials have been sustainably produced and whether the production processes used toxic organic chemicals or heavy metals. Let your mind move to the future – if current trends continue, in ten years' time you will also be buying based on the easy recyclability of your purchases, the environmental consequences of all aspects of the supply chain and the carbon footprint of the manufacturing process.

There is a real, predictable and rapid change going on among organisations that consider themselves leaders. They are demanding higher and higher environmental standards from their suppliers. Sometimes this will seem excessively punctilious, but today's forward-looking manager recognises that this is a trend that companies cannot fight. An organisation buying something even as apparently unimportant as its stationery without a well-informed sense of its environmental impact is soon going to look old-fashioned and irresponsible.

Green stationery catalogues

Much company stationery is bought via large paper catalogues, usually consisting of hundreds of pages of broadly similar products. The last few years have seen the emergence of much smaller catalogues focusing exclusively on stationery items with good green credentials.

One of the new breed of green stationery product lists recently came through my door. (Of course it would make even more sense to offer these products exclusively online, saving the energy costs of making the paper for a catalogue and then sending it out.) BCB Central, a local Oxford-based stationery company, has put all its green product lines into one 48-page booklet. Despite their apparently small size, catalogues such as this one cover most of the ranges needed by smaller offices, including recycled and FSC-certified paper, envelopes, packaging materials and hand towels; recycled staplers and bubble-wrap made from used polythene; Fairtrade and green-certified catering supplies; biodegradable cleaning products and bin liners; and, of course, a wide range of bins to separate office waste for onward recycling.

Water use

With water use generally increasing, supplies from existing reservoirs are becoming more stretched. As a result, water is becoming more and more expensive as the main suppliers have to build ever more costly processing plants. Despite this, few businesses have put in place a robust programme of water-use reduction.

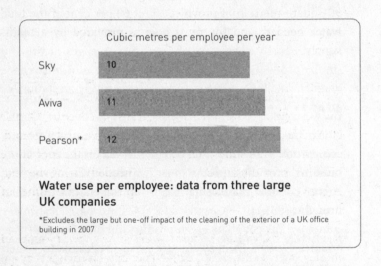

Water use per employee: data from three large UK companies

*Excludes the large but one-off impact of the cleaning of the exterior of a UK office building in 2007

Large UK companies typically use about 10–15 cubic metres of water per year for every employee.

Most specialists say that these figures can be reduced by more than 50 per cent in offices and public buildings; the Environment Agency offers an even higher estimate of about 85 per cent. Most water is used in office kitchens and in toilets. The easiest solutions for cutting consumption are to introduce flush toilets with reduced water use (Interflush, for example) and to use rainwater for providing water for these toilets.

Such systems can make a big difference. New public toilets in the Leicestershire town of Market Bosworth were installed and a rainwater collection system put in place to supply them with water. The toilets use 4.5 litres per flush – up to five times less than in conventional lavatories, and about the lowest figure that is compliant with UK regulations. Water from the 90-square-metre roof provides about 60 per cent of the total water needed, and the remainder is provided by a mains supply.

Southampton University installed a similar rainwater harvesting system for its administration building in 2005. It provides the water for 21 WCs and 3 urinals. It cost just over £4,000 and is expected to pay for itself in five years. An underground, 15,000-litre tank stores rainwater collected off the roof of the building, providing most of the water needed during the year. A conventional mains supply tops up the water in times of drought.

Rainwater harvesting systems won't save huge amounts of money each year (perhaps £20–30 per employee) but they are generally simple to install and are important symbols of good citizenship in a world increasingly short of good-quality water supplies.

The other main option for reducing water use is to use rainwater – or 'grey' water that's been used in basins and showers – for purposes such as watering gardens or lawns. Most plumbers will be able to talk you through the options.

Furniture

A sensible company understands the logic of buying furniture that lasts and maintains its appearance over five, ten or even fifteen years. Also important is the need to buy and use furniture that won't become redundant if office requirements develop, or the business moves into a new building.

Herman Miller, one of the world's leading office furniture manufacturers, has successfully used its environmental credentials to build its corporate image. Few companies around the world have been so successful at linking their brand with environmental sustainability. One vital part of Herman Miller's approach has been to produce furniture that usually looks as though it is at the cutting edge of furniture design, but which very rarely becomes dated or looks out of fashion. A product that is 'sustainable' has to be one that lasts well, and does not rapidly wear out or become visually inappropriate because of changes in fashion or taste.

In its white paper 'Sustainable Products for a Sustainable Planet' (available at www.hmeurope.com), the company explains that it designs its products with three criteria in mind:

- **Material chemistry and safety of inputs** – What chemicals are in the materials specified, and are they the safest available?

- **Disassembly** – Can products be taken apart at the end of their useful life to recycle their materials?

- **Recyclability** – Do the materials contain recycled content and more importantly, can the materials be recycled at the end of the product's useful life?

The first product designed to match the most stringent interpretation of these questions was the redesign of the Mirra™ chair. The company removed plastic components that were difficult to recycle and rethought the chair's structural spine to make it easier to disassemble. Perhaps surprisingly, the net impact of these changes was to reduce the total manufacturing cost of the design.

Herman Miller believes in the McDonough/Braungart manufacturing philosophy, usually known as Cradle to Cradle. This increasingly important approach to design and manufacture emphasises the importance of only using recycled material, and only manufacturing things that then can – and will – be recycled. The outcome of this approach is almost zero waste and minimal degradation of the environment, either through pollution or through over-use of resources.

Herman Miller makes modernist furniture that is built to last. Luke Hughes & Co (www.lukehughes.co.uk) is a specialist wooden furniture manufacturer headquartered in Covent Garden, London, with a slightly different approach. It makes ranges of chairs and tables for customers who insist on durability and timelessness. It has sold its products to 54 out of the 68 Oxford and Cambridge colleges as well as to cathedrals, boardrooms and government offices. Look at the furniture and you are in little doubt that it will survive decades of intense use and still remain fit for its purpose. The word 'sustainability' barely features on the company's website, and it makes only very limited claims for the origins of the wood it sources. (As the Timbmet story on p. 279 shows, guaranteeing that timber is genuinely sustainable is not easy.) The furniture is expensive but uses virtually no metal or plastic components.

With its design ethos clearly still tied to the 19th century Arts and Crafts movement, is this company (and its products) 'green'? I would suggest it is. A business that uses renewable materials and turns them into products that will last for hundreds of years is actually as green a company as one can get. Although Herman Miller and Luke Hughes & Co could not be more different as businesses, they are each working towards a green ideal.

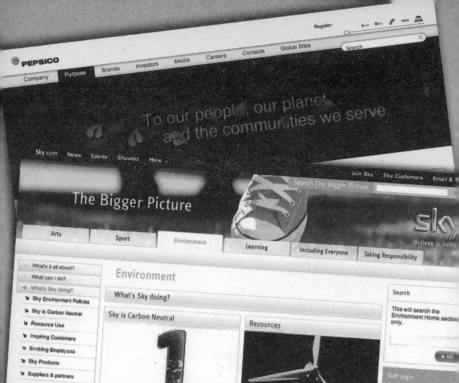

To our people, our planet and the communities we serve.

PEPSICO

Company | Purpose | Brands | Investors | Media | Careers | Contacts | Global Sites | Search

Sky.com | News | Sports | Showbiz | More

Join Sky | Sky Customers | Email & T

The Bigger Picture

sky

Believe in bette

Arts | Sport | Environment | Learning | Including Everyone | Taking Responsibility

Environment

- What's it all about?
- What can I do?
- → What's Sky doing?
- ✗ Sky Environment Policies
- ✗ Sky is Carbon Neutral
- ✗ Resource Use
- ✗ Inspiring Customers
- ✗ Enabling Employees
- ✗ Sky Products
- ✗ Suppliers & partners
- ✗ Frequently Asked Questions
- ✗ Global Action Plan
- ✗ Al Gore's UK Message
- ✗ Sky and the Environment

What's Sky doing?

Sky is Carbon Neutral

Sky became the world's first Carbon Neutral media company in 2006.

✗ Learn how Sky did this.

Resources

From energy efficient buildings to recycling, Sky is working hard to make its operations as environmentally friendly as possible.

✗ Read more

Inspiring customers

At Sky we want to inspire our customers to live more sustainably.

✗ Find out how Sky is inspiring its consumers.

Enabling employees

Our people and our environmental initiatives - working together.

✗ Find out how Sky is enabling its employees.

Search

This will search the Environment Home section only.

✗ GO

Staff Login

Access your Bigger Picture Card by entering your staff email address:

Enter Password:

✗ GO

- ✗ Register now
- ✗ Forgotten your password?

Environment news

Sky is partnering The Climate Group and other businesses to launch the 'Together.com' campaign

✗ Find out more

Did you know?

Over 20,000 people have

Communicating your environmental successes and failures is an important part of the task.

Presenting your green credentials

What you say may be as important as what you do

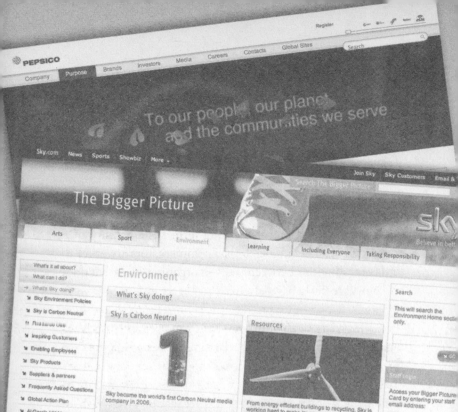

To our people, our planet
and the communities we serve

Sky.com   News   Sports   Showbiz   More ▾

Join Sky   Sky Customers   Email 8

The Bigger Picture

Search The Bigger Picture

sky

Believe in bett

Arts   Sport   Environment   Learning   Including Everyone   Taking Responsibility

What's it all about?
What can I do?
→ What's Sky doing?
▾ Sky Environment Policies
▾ Sky is Carbon Neutral
▾ Plasticube Club
▾ Inspiring Customers
▾ Enabling Employees
▾ Sky Products
▾ Suppliers & partners
▾ Frequently Asked Questions
▾ Global Action Plan
▾ Al Gore's UK Message
▾ Sky and the Environment

Environment

What's Sky doing?

Sky is Carbon Neutral

Sky became the world's first Carbon Neutral media company in 2006.

▾ Learn how Sky did this.

Resources

From energy efficient buildings to recycling, Sky is working hard to make its operations as environmentally friendly as possible.

▾ Read more

Inspiring customers

At Sky we want to inspire our customers to live more sustainably.

▾ Find out how Sky is inspiring its consumers.

Enabling employees

Our people and our environmental initiatives - working together.

▾ Find out how Sky is enabling its employees.

Search

This will search the Environment Home section only.

▾ GO

Access your Bigger Picture Card by entering your staff email address:

Enter Password:

▾ GO

▾ Register now
▾ Forgotten your password?

Sky is partnering The Climate Group and other businesses to launch the 'Together.com' campaign

▾ Find out more

Did you know?

Over 20,000 people have calculated their carbon footprint using Sky's Carbon Calculator

▾ Calculate your carbon

The stance an organisation takes on green issues is likely to be interesting to its stakeholders. Investors, for example, are taking increasing note of the long-term sustainability of a company's business model. Media commentators are eager to find contradictions between what an organisation says it does and how it really behaves. In this chapter we look at how well-regarded companies have chosen to present details of how they are facing green issues, and the advantages and disadvantages of carbon labelling and offsetting. We examine the case for 'choice editing' – ceasing to sell goods or services that are environmentally unfriendly in use. We then look at how to avoid being perceived as untruthful because of 'greenwash' in advertising or promotional activities, and conclude by looking at how two companies dealt successfully with pressure from green activists.

Annual reports on green issues

In the last few years, Sky and PepsiCo have focused on developing green policies that are both effective and also help build the public image of their companies and products. Let's look at what they concentrate on, what they measure and how successful they have been. Most importantly, where are the pitfalls? What works and what doesn't?

Sky

Jeremy Darroch, the CEO of Sky, recently wrote:

I believe that a successful and sustainable business is a responsible business; one that does the right thing, sees the bigger picture and works hard to tackle the issues that its people and customers care about.

Sky doesn't put its efforts to improve the green characteristics of the company in a separate box to its other good citizenship activities. Reducing the electricity consumption of its set-top boxes sits alongside corporate volunteering and increasing participation in sport in Sky's listing of its corporate activities – training 5,500 amateur cricket coaches is part of the same programme as reducing the company's carbon footprint.

Sky's climate-change programme has five strands:

- Inspiring its customers to take action
- Multiplying its actions in partnership with others
- Reducing its own carbon footprint
- Using less and recycling more
- Getting employees and suppliers to improve their environmental performance.

Inspiring customers

Sky has nine million customers, and is present in over a third of the UK's homes. Each home has a set-top box. Older generations of these boxes have been greedy users of electricity when in use. They also had limited ability to go into an energy-efficient standby mode. Sky sees that it is no use proclaiming itself to be an environmentally aware company if its customers are landed with electronic appliances that add perhaps 5 per cent to their electricity bill. It doesn't take a genius to work out that Sky's most important impact on the environment arises from customers using its products. So beginning in 2007, all Sky's new boxes have had lower power consumption and a software improvement that shifts them automatically into low-power mode if they are not being used after 11 p.m.

Simply by installing these efficient new boxes for some of its customers, Sky has saved more CO_2 than the direct footprint of its own company operations. As the new technology is rolled out across all its customers, the savings from this change will come to dwarf those that can be made within the company itself. This is an important rule – a company can often make more greenhouse-gas reductions from focusing on how its customers use its products than it can by small improvements in its own performance. An architect practice designing a new school powered by solar energy, or a retailer selling clothes that can be washed at low temperatures, do more for the country's carbon emissions than by making tweaks in their own electricity consumption. It is, however, far more difficult to attract favourable press attention by improving other people's carbon footprint than your own.

Partnerships with others

Sky's primary partner is an inspiring and unusual environmental charity. Global Action Plan aims to get employees and customers to engage in worthwhile and enjoyable projects that help save energy and reduce costs. Sky has focused on two particular activities in the past year – a sustainable food progamme for schools and Global Action Plan's flagship 'Eco-Teams' project. The Eco-Teams idea gets people to work together in groups to discuss major environmental issues and work together to reduce waste, energy, water use and travel. Sky employees will be trained to run their own Eco-Teams and the company says it hopes to reduce their household carbon footprints by 15 per cent as well as save water and cut down on waste. Their website – www.jointhebiggerpicture.com – is a good example of how to engage employees.

Global Action Plan demonstrates the importance of using specialist and enthusiastic outside help. Even though Sky is one of the most environmentally aware companies in the UK, it probably didn't have the internal experience to build employee commitment to green actions. Sky's interesting choice of long-term charity partner also shows the primary importance of getting a company's staff deeply involved in supporting the drive to better environmental performance. E.ON, one of Global Action Plan's other clients, put it succinctly:

If you haven't got your own people convinced you might as well pack up and go home – and Global Action Plan was an incredibly powerful way of us doing it.

Reducing its own carbon footprint

Sky is one of those ambitious organizations that has promised to run its entire operation as 'carbon neutral'. This means that it buys carbon offsets for the emissions that it cannot otherwise avoid, investing mainly in wind and hydro projects in Asia.

Sky's claim to be carbon neutral was questioned by

complainants to the Advertising Standards Authority (ASA). The ASA investigated and found that Sky's statement was fair – it had actually gone further than it needed to in measuring its emissions and appropriately offsetting them. Sky says it was important that its data was all externally verified by an independent expert – if the ASA had found against Sky, much of the company's growing reputation for environmental leadership would have been instantly eroded. The key lesson for other companies is – don't make claims that won't stand up to critical scrutiny. Get found out and the cost to the business will almost certainly be far greater than any benefit obtained.

Sky also declares its carbon footprint calculations before offsetting; 2007 saw a rise for the first time since detailed measurements began, with the company blaming increasing car travel and the operations of its fleet of vans. Many companies slightly complicate the reporting of their emissions by presenting the data in terms of tonnes per employee or per point of revenue. Sky does not do this, so the natural increase in emissions arising from business growth will always tend to show the company in an unfavourable light. But it means that it has to prepare itself for criticism of failing to restrain its own emissions even as it proclaims itself a green organisation.

Another way of looking at emissions is to calculate them per employee. Each one of Sky's people is indirectly responsible for about 4 tonnes of greenhouse gases. As with most businesses, the most important source is electricity use which accounts for almost one and a half tonnes. Average usage was about 13,000 kilowatt hours per person, about four times the usage of the typical entire household. And if Sky had not bought renewable, zero-carbon energy to cover most of these needs, the carbon-dioxide output from this would have been over 5 tonnes per person. In future, government guidelines will require companies not to account for renewable energy as zero-carbon. The UK's Climate Change Committee is now saying that total emissions across all personal and business activities, as well as all fuels, need to decline to no more than about 2 tonnes, so we can see that Sky still has a long way to go. Of course, it needs plenty of power for television studios and for its server farms. But these figures show that even a company as resolute and thoughtful as Sky faces an enormous battle to get emissions down to a sustainable level.

Using less and recycling more

Sky removed all under-desk rubbish bins from its Scottish sites this year. Making it more difficult to just throw things away often has important benefits in reducing waste. Water use was also down – to about 10 tonnes per person.

Getting customers to recycle their equipment is a more important challenge. The company recycled about 800,000 pieces of electronics in 2007, with engineers visiting the homes taking back equipment that wasn't needed. Customers are much less likely to take action themselves. Although Sky provides bags with free postage for returning items that are no longer needed, only 5,000 customers took advantage of the offer. People will generally say that they are very committed to recycling everything that they can, but their behaviour will often fail to match this promise.

Getting suppliers and employees to improve their own environmental performance

Most corporate audits of carbon footprints, including Sky's, don't include the emissions from employees driving to work. They probably should. In fact, it is difficult to see why a commuter journey is any less the responsibility of a company than a van delivery driver carrying the business's products. Both vehicles are making journeys that the company needs.

Sky does, however, have an active policy of encouraging public transport use, providing grants for the purchase of hybrid cars and discounts on bikes. It also runs a lift-sharing site and operates a company shuttle bus service between its main west London office and the local tube stations.

In addition, Sky actively maintains a website that carries news on climate change issues as well as giving advice on low-carbon living. It promotes video-conferencing, although unlike some companies it doesn't say how much its expensive suites are used. Interestingly for such a large company, Sky makes no mention of encouraging working from home, possibly the single best way of reducing carbon emissions from employee travel.

PepsiCo

PepsiCo in the UK and Ireland is an unusually sensitive organisation with a full programme of policies to try to minimise its impact on the environment. It controls UK businesses that make potato crisps (Walkers), oat products (Quaker), Tropicana Copella fruit juices and PJ's Smoothies, as well as the core cola brand. To an extent that is not well understood, food and drink companies are at the centre of environmental issues. Agriculture is probably responsible for a fifth of global emissions. The refrigerants used in chilled food and drink cabinets are some of the most potent of industrial global warming gases, far worse than CO_2. It is not surprising that some of the best work on 'greening' organisations comes from companies like PepsiCo and Coca-Cola.

Even more than other food products companies, worldwide soft-drink brands are aware of environmental issues. They are working in tropical countries with major concerns over the long-term availability of clean drinking water. Bottling soft drinks can use very large quantities of this scarce resource, and environmental activists have rightly targeted the global companies that dominate this industry. As a result, water use has improved dramatically and Coca-Cola has now committed to being 'water-neutral' in some of its driest markets.

This section focuses on Pepsi UK and Ireland. Its first Environmental Sustainability Report is one of the most all-embracing and thoughtful documents produced by a large company. The business case for taking environmental issues very seriously is eloquently made:

Natural resources are vital for our business as well as the planet. Our products completely depend on agriculture, which depends in turn on a certain climate (which forests significantly regulate), water provision, and fertile land to grow crops successfully. In addition almost every single stage of our supply chain is currently dependent on fossil fuel.

The Report lists Pepsi UK's achievements during the last few years. These focus on:

- Energy reduction. Walkers Crisps energy use fell by 32 per cent per standard packet between 2000 and 2007. And Quaker buys 100 per cent renewable energy.

- Measurement. No organisation can manage its footprint downwards without accurate measurement and monitoring. Surprisingly few organisations realise this and many continue to publish data on environmental issues that is transparently wrong or incomplete. Pepsi UK's procedures are clear and extremely robust. This is what made it possible to put the Carbon Label on its crisp packets in 2007.

- Pepsi UK realises that most of the emissions embedded in its products are not within its direct control. It is now taking an active part in helping to manage the emissions in its own supply chain and in sponsoring research into the wider issues of how to reduce emissions among suppliers.

- Pepsi UK has also focused on reducing the weight of its packaging and the amount of energy used in its manufacture – 2007 saw an 18 per cent reduction in the amount of plastic used in a Tropicana bottle.

- Previously unused starch from potatoes at the crisp factory is now 'recycled' into other snacks.

- Water used in cola manufacture fell by 39 per cent per bottle between 2003 and 2007.

The company's pledges for the next few years include:

- A striking commitment to send no waste to landfill by 2017. This promise is not just for the company itself, but also for all its suppliers.

- To reduce energy use per unit of production by a further 2 per cent within three years.

- To use only renewable energy across all its UK operations within 15 years.

- That all Quaker and Walkers packaging is to be 'renewable, recyclable or biodegradable' within ten years.

- A 45 per cent reduction in water use within three years.

These are extremely demanding targets, particularly for a company that has already been focused on sustainability objectives for several years.

The report recognises the underlying tension between running a growing business and reducing the impact on the environment. It is not enough to reduce the kilogrammes of emissions per unit of product – in a fast-growing business, greenhouse gases will still be going up. Instead, the focus must be on unlinking emissions from manufacture so that absolute levels of resource use fall even as the business grows. Pepsi UK puts it this way:

We, and others, need to commit to renewable energy, improved agricultural practices, less intensive packaging materials, and identifying other transformational ways of doing business. We need to find a way to separate developing great new products and growing the business from an ever-increasing burden on the natural world.

Salman Amin, President, PepsiCo UK & Ireland

Pepsi UK also places unusual emphasis on putting a management structure in place that ensures that green issues are robustly addressed.

We have Site Sustainability Managers in place at all our manufacturing sites, a Central Sustainability Team, and are developing an Environmental Management System. We have implemented internal metrics and scorecards, have 100% corporate reporting on energy and water, and all plants will be ISO 14001 accredited by the end of 2008.

(ISO 14001 is a set of principles for environmental management, and organisations intending to pursue green objectives may find it worthwhile to get accredited. ISO 14001 costs money and management time, but helps build an organisation's skills and commitment. It also helps persuade potential customers that the company takes environmental issues seriously.)

Much of the Environmental Sustainability Report's emphasis is on helping suppliers to manage their own impact. Tropicana's juice all comes from a family-owned orange plantation in Brazil, and Pepsi UK also reports on the actions taken by this business to limit its impact on the local ecology.

There is much less in the Report on how Pepsi UK helps to manage the emissions of its customers. One of the most important issues facing soft-drink companies is minimising the global warming impact of the leakage of particularly potent gases from the chilling system of their soft-drinks cabinets. At the moment, almost all soft-drink chillers contain gases called HFCs or HCFCs, both of which are extremely bad from a climate change point of view. Some of these gases are several thousand times worse than carbon dioxide. But this topic only gets a short paragraph in the 40-page document. It acknowledges the importance of the issue, but its statements are more unspecific than the other concrete promises in this very impressive Report.

Also missing is any substantive discussion of how Pepsi UK might reduce the net impact of its activities by improving the recycling of its soft-drink bottles and cans. The UK recycling infrastructure is weak and insufficient, so Pepsi UK and other organisations that are indirectly responsible for much consumer waste need to be more active in working out how to improve the availability of easy recycling. This means a sustained (and costly) effort to find ways in which private enterprise can build profitable and large recycling businesses.

Any reader of the Pepsi UK Report will be struck by the willingnesss of the company to discuss the main issues it now faces when it addresses resource use and climate change. It identifies five specific dilemmas that demonstrate how difficult companies will find it to be truly green while still continuing to reward shareholders and give employees well-paid and satisfying jobs:

- How do we continue to grow our business but reduce our absolute environmental impacts?

- Faced with competitive pressures, how do companies collaborate through their supply chains on carbon management?

- How do we respond to demands from consumers or retailers that might increase our carbon footprint?

- Should sourcing be shifted away from water-stressed regions or countries, or should suppliers be engaged to reduce their water footprint?

- Does the consumer focus on packaging risk diverting attention from larger environmental goals?

The last question is one that recurs frequently among

manufacturers making consumer goods. Most of Pepsi UK's impact is not from its packaging but from its agricultural supply. Only 15 per cent of the carbon footprint of a bag of crisps comes from its packaging, with a small amount also allocated to the carbon cost of disposing of cardboard cases. How potatoes are grown is far more important, but consumers are far less interested in this issue. UK manufacturers and retailers need to work together to identify, acknowledge and publicise the importance of agricultural emissions as opposed to those arising from the manufacture and disposal of packaging.

Pepsi UK's impressive sustainability report is one of relatively few in the UK that acknowledge that a responsible business will need to work extremely hard to make the radical emissions cuts that are required. But the business sees the benefits of pitching itself as one of the clear innovators. The company writes:

Today's consumers increasingly view their spending decisions as a way to make a difference in the world. They want to see their values reflected in the products they buy and their communities strengthened by the businesses they support. At PepsiCo, we are in a good position to take on this challenge.

Full carbon disclosure – Patagonia

Despite the US government's previous lack of interest in green policy-making, some US companies lead the world in environmental policies. The best businesses disclose more about their manufacturing processes and their carbon footprint than almost any European or Asian companies. One of the best examples is Patagonia, a highly regarded maker of specialist outdoor clothing. To jaded European eyes, its environmental plans look almost embarrassingly earnest and idealistic. The admissions of its own weaknesses are delivered with a humility that we rarely see on this side of the Atlantic. What UK business would voluntarily describe the production processes of one of its key products as 'not sustainable'? Or admit that a complex chemical in the water repellant used in its outer garments (and those of all its competitors) is highly persistent and building up in the environment?

Patagonia's latest innovation is to document the full environmental impact of five of its products. Part of the company's website is devoted to analysing each stage in the production of these standard items. A polo shirt is tracked from the organic cotton farm in Turkey to the spinning factory in Thailand, eventually ending up in a warehouse in Nevada. From the cotton field to the warehouse is 14,000 miles. Patagonia says the CO_2 produced is 40 times the weight of the garment. The energy taken to make and transport the polo shirt could have been used to run a low-energy light bulb non-stop for 77 days. The waste involved in getting the product to the consumer is as great as the weight of the garment. If the polo shirt looks bad, the woollen sweater is even worse – the energy used to make this product would power the average US household for 20 hours.

The average UK shopper buys about 35 kg of clothes a year, not very different from the US consumer. If Patagonia's figures are correct, our clothes purchases account for at least a tonne of global warming gases a year, or not far off 10 per cent of our total carbon footprint. For a clothing company to openly advertise the high environmental costs of its products is brave indeed.

Patagonia has also allowed its customers to comment on its manufacturing processes. Some of the comments are highly critical, but remain on the website for others to see. Customers complain about the chromium used to tan its shoes, or question why Patagonia's polyester products still contain antimony. Others attack the company's motives, or criticise it for producing almost all its clothes in the Far East. The comments are patiently answered and the company's flaws candidly acknowledged. The openness and apparently genuine transparency seem to stem from a view that Patagonia can admit to its mistakes and still have a far better environmental image than its competitors.

Anyone reading the Patagonia site must take away a message that clothing manufacture is far more environmentally damaging than its relatively benign image suggests. The true costs are hidden from view in a Chinese factory or a Bangkok spinning mill. Patagonia acknowledges this, almost implying that we might actually choose to buy fewer items. Only a company with a deep self-confidence could possibly suggest that customers should defer buying its products.

Patagonia's mission statement openly acknowledges that the world faces 'an environmental crisis'. Unlike the many companies that have built a veneer of environmental respectability and then made exaggerated claims for their virtue, it simply says 'as yet, there is no such thing as a sustainable business'.

As a privately owned company, Patagonia can perhaps more easily afford to pursue a strategy of genuine environmental transparency. Its customers will almost always be loyal buyers who love wild open spaces, and who have noticed the creeping impact of climate change and environmental despoliation on the places they love. Nevertheless, it seems a risky business strategy to identify the severe impacts of your manufacturing processes and to be willing to openly engage with critical customers. But I was convinced. I know that next time I need to buy outdoor clothing I will be actively looking out for the Patagonia label. As ethical considerations become more important to the British consumer, UK companies should think about following Patagonia's painfully honest lead.

Carbon labelling

A brief flurry of interest greeted the announcement in spring 2007 that packets of Walkers' crisps would carry a new carbon label. The standard 35-gramme packet of the cheese and onion variety now has a sign saying that the CO_2 emissions resulting from the production of the crisps was 75 grammes (or over two times as much as the weight of the snack).

Other major firms promised to build on the Walkers experiment: Tesco said it would label many of its food products, and Innocent Smoothies calculated the carbon from some of its drinks. But progress since the first announcements has been very slow. Behind the small label on the crisp packet are a host of tough issues. It is relatively easy to work out the footprint of an office but fiendishly complicated to go back up the supply chain to calculate the full carbon cost of all the activities that need to take place to put even something as simple as a packet of crisps on a supermarket shelf.

The lesson for business? Don't get distracted by carbon

labelling. The costs are high and it may well be better to focus on reducing emissions rather than trying to measure them to excessively high degrees of accuracy. If your customers want to know the greenhouse-gas consequences of your products, give them good estimates but don't waste huge sums of money trying to give them a precise figure.

Walkers' label

We've already commented on how much energy Walkers Crisps has saved. It also reduced its water use by over 50 per cent between 2001 and 2007. In addition, the Carbon Trust found some other surprising ways that Walkers saved energy. Potatoes are sold by weight, so farmers keep them in humid conditions so they don't lose water, making them lighter. But frying a potato uses more energy when it contains a lot of water, so from Walkers' point of view it is better to store the potatoes in a dry place, where their water content will gradually decline. It makes far more sense for the crisp company to pay a slightly higher price per tonne to its farmers, in return for its suppliers not storing their products in a humid atmosphere.

The carbon label was an outcome of the Carbon Trust's work. The Trust calculated the emissions from each part of the production process. It found that almost half the greenhouse gases were produced on the farm.

Walkers was initially extremely enthusiastic about the label on its crisps and said that it would roll out the idea to its other flavours. Progress seems to have stalled, perhaps as ▶

the costs and complexity of the analysis needed for each
different type of crisp became increasingly apparent.

44 per cent	On the farm
30 per cent	Energy used in manufacturing
15 per cent	Energy used to make packaging
9 per cent	Transport to retailers
2 per cent	Disposal of packaging
Total	**75 grammes of CO_2 and other greenhouse gases**

What is carbon labelling actually trying to do?

The companies and research organisations backing carbon
labelling have very considerable ambitions for their ideas.
They want to achieve two important objectives:

- To give consumers an objective way of comparing different
  products. A satisfactory labelling system will give people the
  opportunity to choose the brands with the lowest carbon
  footprint.

- To show companies (and their customers) where the greenhouse gases really come from. It surprised people that
  growing the potato crop creates far more emissions than
  actually processing and cooking the crisps or packaging them
  into cardboard boxes full of little foil packets. Armed with
  this information, organisations can work to reduce their
  energy use. Companies using a carbon label commit to year-
  on-year reductions in energy use and greenhouse-gas output.

These are fine objectives. Some consumers have a high level of interest in carbon reduction and will actively seek out products that they know are reliably better than others in this respect. But many customers found the first wave of carbon labels deeply confusing. They couldn't quite see the point of the 75-gramme figure on the cheese and onion crisp packet. Was this figure a lot or a little? Would it be better to buy another flavour or the products of another company?

Many people questioned how a 35-gramme bag of crisps could possibly embody 75 grammes of CO_2. In some ways, this reaction was a useful one. Very few people realise how important food production and processing is in creating greenhouse-gas emissions, so Walkers was bringing an important issue to the fore. However, the overall effect of carbon labels appears to be quite unhelpful in assisting ordinary consumers to understand how their purchases affect CO_2 emissions. This is partly because there are so few labels.

For a business seeking to understand how and where its production processes, and those of its suppliers, add to emissions, a carbon label can be a better idea. If energy is going to become more and more expensive, then it clearly makes good sense to know where it is used. Like the Walkers potatoes, is most of the energy embodied in your products actually expended by your suppliers? How important is packaging, for example? An organisation understanding the answer to these questions will be better equipped to drive down carbon emissions along the entire chain, from raw materials to customers. So although actually putting a printed label on packaging may not be a good idea, working out the carbon contained in a product or service is definitely a good idea.

Thus far, the research necessary to generate a reliable figure for a manufactured product has been eye-wateringly expensive – a single product might cost £50,000 or more. Many manufacturers are unimpressed by the whole idea of carbon labels. Procter and Gamble wrote:

Based on P&G's experiences over the past 20 years, we believe that eco-seal (carbon-labelling) programs have numerous problems, and that they neither encourage environmental progress nor empower consumers.

Why is it so difficult?

Most people are now concluding the expense of a fully certified carbon label is not worth the research effort or the money it costs. But why is it quite so difficult?

- Most products and services in the modern economy involve a complex chain of suppliers. An item of packaged food might contain 30 or 40 ingredients and almost all of these will have already been substantially processed by the time they arrive at the manufacturer. Even a very simple item like a ball-point pen involves tens of different suppliers, each with their own chain of suppliers. Something like a commercial wind turbine contains 8,000 parts, many made in small factories in Asia. Tracing back to the original metals and plastics is inevitably extremely complex.

- There is never any clear boundary to where the calculation stops. It may be possible to calculate how much diesel and fertiliser a potato farmer uses, but the farmer also needs to buy the seed potatoes he or she requires to grow the crop.

Should these also be included in the calculation? And the seed potatoes from which these came?

Should we include the carbon costs of the product when in use? Boots puts a carbon label on some of its hair shampoos. The carbon cost of making shampoo is tiny compared to the energy used in heating the water for a shower. Is the Boots label actually providing any useful information?

Carbon offsetting

Almost all activities – business and personal – generate carbon dioxide. Even after an organisation has taken all the reasonable steps it can to reduce its greenhouse-gas emissions, it will still be a producer of greenhouse gases. Companies can decide to reduce their footprint still further by buying carbon 'offsets'. Or a business can decide to use offsets to neutralise the carbon impact of particular events, such as a rock concert or corporate away-day.

Offsets are sold by specialist companies that control projects elsewhere in the world that systematically reduce emissions. Some companies buy enough offsets to completely neutralise the global warming effect of all their activities; Sky and some of the main high-street banks are good examples. Other organisations and individuals just offset part of their emissions. They might, for example, only offset the effect of their air travel. A small number of businesses have also chosen to buy reductions that counter-balance the emissions of the products they make after they have been sold to customers. Land Rover is one example – it offsets the emissions of its vehicles on the road, typically for about two years of use.

Offsetting is growing fast, particularly in the US. There, companies are not covered by mandatory emissions caps but many have decided that it is responsible to reduce their net emissions anyway. Offsetting has had many critics over the last few years – including the author of this book – but our comments are becoming much more muted as the offsetting industry becomes more professional and strives to improve the quality of the carbon-reduction projects around the world. One estimate is that 10 million tonnes of greenhouse gases were offset in 2006, but the number is now probably several times that.

Offsetting is a complicated business, with a host of different approaches and standards. We will try to unpack some of the complexities below, but first let's look at a simple example of how it works.

Counter-balancing corporate air travel

A company – let's call it Walton Educational Services – calculates that the emissions resulting from the air travel of its employees amount to about 1,000 tonnes per year as it serves its customers in the Far East and Europe. (Some travel agents can make these calculations for you.) One of Walton's customers is a government agency that is asking its suppliers to demonstrate commitment to emissions reduction. After careful study, the company decides that it should be able to reduce emissions from flights to about 600 tonnes by careful selection of airlines, switching to rail travel and a greater use of video-conferencing. It decides to offset this 600 tonnes by voluntarily buying offsets.

It goes to Climate Care, one of the UK's top providers of high-quality offsets. Based in Oxford, but also with offices in Kenya, Chile and Turkey, Climate Care has been in the business for over ten years and has unrivalled experience of building good carbon-cutting projects in the developing world. The people in Kenya and elsewhere spend their time looking for large-scale ways of systematically and measurably reducing emissions.

Climate Care offers prospective customers a list of six or so potential investments. These range from efficient cooking stoves in Uganda to wind projects in China. It's probably obvious why a new wind turbine cuts carbon emissions, but you may be unsure about cooking stoves. Traditional open fires waste a lot of fuel, so the idea is that a family with a metal- or brick-enclosed stove will use less wood to cook their food. This reduces the pressure to cut down trees. So this project qualifies as an offset because it avoids deforestation – one fewer tree cut down means hundreds of kilos of CO_2 kept out of the global atmosphere.

The company chooses the Ugandan stove project. It likes the fact that it can identify the communities in which the stoves are installed, whereas the effects of the Chinese wind projects are slightly less easy to see. When it talks about its offsetting, Walton feels that its staff and customers will be more impressed by a scheme in rural Uganda. This is not a foolish consideration – there's nothing wrong with choosing a project that will look good to stakeholders as well as reducing emissions.

Climate Care has done its calculations. From watching how the stoves are used in real life, it is able to assess how many tonnes of wood are saved each year compared to traditional cooking techniques. Perhaps a stove reduces wood consumption by the equivalent of one tonne of CO_2 a year and the stove is expected to last ten years. Each stove therefore reduces carbon-dioxide emissions by ten tonnes. Typically, a high-quality wood cooking stove costs approximately £50, meaning that the cost per tonne of carbon dioxide saved is about £5.

Climate Care currently charges the company slightly more, since it needs to cover its overheads and make a reasonable profit. Its price is £7.50 plus VAT per tonne of offset. With the money, Climate Care will make sure that sufficient extra stoves are sold in Uganda to counter-balance 600 tonnes of air travel. That might mean about 60 stoves that wouldn't otherwise have been installed. The company gets a certificate to show its clients that it has offset all its air travel and a sense that its money is probably very well employed on a carbon-reduction scheme in a poor country.

What to look for when buying offsets

Your customers might be forcing you into purchasing carbon offsets, in which case you may not care much how effective your money is at reducing emissions elsewhere in the world. But the ethically managed company will also want to be sure that its money is being well spent. Is your cash really going to a good project? And will this scheme actually cut emissions by the amount claimed? Does it have any beneficial effects on the local community? You could spend months checking out how exactly your money is being used, but you probably only really need to think about four important issues:

● *Is the project certified by a reputable authority?*

All but the largest companies will usually be buying what are called 'voluntary' carbon offsets. (They may not seem voluntary if you know you have to buy them to impress customers or government.) The best voluntary projects will usually be certified by one of two or three bodies. The Gold Standard is a Swiss-based body that has set up a standard by which the quality of a project is measured. A carbon offset scheme with a Gold Standard label will have been independently verified – it will either work by improving energy efficiency (such as advanced cooking stoves) or by funding renewable energy projects (such as wind turbines in China). It must also help to improve local living conditions. The other main certification bodies used by carbon offset companies in the UK are called VCS (Voluntary Carbon Standard) or VER+. If the project in which you are investing carries these labels, then you can be reasonably sure that it is worthwhile.

The very largest offset projects in the world usually come under what is called the Clean Development Mechanism (CDM). The CDM was set up to allow trade in carbon allowances. If a company, such as a power station operator, is only allowed to produce 10 million tonnes of CO_2, but actually produces 11 million tonnes, it can in certain circumstances buy a 1-million-tonne CDM project in the developing world and say it has met its obligations. Judged on a net basis, its emissions are reduced to its cap of 10 million tonnes. CDM projects typically include large hydro-electric dams and schemes to reduce the output of potent industrial greenhouse gases from Chinese factories. Many people have severe doubts about CDM projects, and the commentator Oliver Tickell recently pointed out that most of them would have been carried out anyway, so there was no net reduction of emissions. However, the UK government is more optimistic and recommends the use of CDM projects for offsetting.

Expect the very best projects to have a higher price per tonne of emission. This is simply a question of supply and demand. Everyone wants to back the really good schemes that have a tangible effect on emissions, so people can charge more for them; prices over £15 a tonne are not unusual.

- *Does the project look as though it genuinely reduces emissions?*

This is a much trickier question than it seems. It is almost impossible to be certain that the project in which you invested money would not have happened anyway, without the support of a carbon-offset company. Remember the Ugandan cooking stove example offered by Climate Care? Who can know whether the families would have bought a new stove anyway, because it saved having to buy expensive fuel or collect more wood from a remote forest? Or perhaps an international aid agency would have purchased the stoves. The Chinese wind turbine is even more problematic. Putting up wind turbines is a profitable investment in windy parts of the world. So the carbon offset money may be achieving no additional effect.

Second, it is extremely difficult to actually assess the emissions reduction from a project. A family with a new efficient stove may be more profligate with the use of wood or the savings may be less than expected. These may seem academic points, but they are not. If carbon offsets don't work, then we are kidding ourselves that we can continue to produce as much CO_2 in the developed economies. If there are no reliable ways of offsetting our emissions, rich economies will need to cut their emissions even faster and more sharply than we expect.

- *Is the project outside the countries covered by mandatory emissions caps from the Kyoto Protocol?*

Many people would prefer to invest in carbon-reduction projects in their own country. One senior Marks & Spencer executive once said to me that he would rather his company spent money insulating the homes of its UK employees than sending it to remote areas where there is no check that the money is being invested properly. But, perhaps paradoxically, insulating UK homes may not result in carbon reductions. In the UK we are obliged by the Kyoto Protocol to hold our emissions below a certain level and the government has put policies in place to achieve this aim. If M&S cut UK fuel use by improving home insulation, the government can relax these policies by a small amount and still keep within the Kyoto limits. This means that carrying out offsetting in European countries is frowned upon, and will generally not be accepted by bodies seeking to assure themselves that offsets are genuine.

- *Will your customers and employees approve of the project?*

One of the great values of proper offsetting is that it impresses your stakeholders. The better the project, the greater the effect. It may be worth having a straw poll among your employees as to the best scheme to back.

What are the possible downsides from offsetting?

One of the principal criticisms of offsetting is that it encourages the organisation or individual to continue with unsustainable fossil-fuel use; critics fear that offsetting encourages people to continue wasting energy, clearing their consciences by investing in appealing projects in the third world.

The evidence on whether this is true is mixed. Among individuals, offsetting is unlikely to encourage profligacy. The small percentage of people who use offsetting for air travel have shown by their willingness to spend money that they are much more sensitive to global-warming issues than their peers. It seems implausible that their attitude will be 'since I offset all my flights, I can take an extra trip to New York'. For organisations, it is not quite as clear. Even at the top price of £15 or more per tonne, offsetting may well be very much cheaper than investments in energy saving in offices, shops and factories. The existence of the offsetting safety valve may encourage a little slackness in really pursuing greenhouse-gas reductions inside the organisation.

Barclays has a very interesting approach. It charges each business unit for offsetting based on the emissions it produces. Any capital investment appraisals for energy efficiency measures then include the savings from not having to pay this internal charge. This makes efficiency measures slightly easier to justify and has, for example, tipped the balance in favour of better video-conferencing equipment. Charging a business unit for the costs of offsetting its activities has also got managers used to paying for carbon for the first time.

Another potential problem is that offsetting is widely

distrusted by environmental activists and many journalists. They believe that many offset schemes are little better than fraudulent. Poor-quality projects pushed by the offset firms have had bad publicity in the press. If your organisation had backed these initiatives, your reputation would have suffered.

Offsets and air travel

Offsetting air travel needs particular care. An aircraft produces CO_2 as it burns jet fuel but also emits other pollutants in the high atmosphere that add to global warming. As page 195 explains, we do not yet know exactly how much extra warming is caused by aviation. Some people think that we should be cautious and multiply the effect of the carbon dioxide by three to get a realistic figure for the full effect of aviation, while others are more optimistic and point to recent evidence that air travel might be slightly less detrimental than we used to think. They would suggest that a multiplier of two is more accurate.

Why does this matter? Some offsetting companies only include the effect of CO_2 in their calculation of how many tonnes of offsetting are needed to provide a counter-weight to air travel. This is not enough – the offset provider must make a clear and explicit statement about the assumptions it uses for the effect of other greenhouse gases coming from the jet engines.

For some companies, aviation is the most important single source of greenhouse-gas emissions. So deciding which carbon offsetting company to use is particularly important. The sensible thing to do is to ask exactly how the offset provider calculates the effect of aviation and for the scientific data it uses to support its assumptions. Good companies will respond properly and the sharks will not return your call.

Alternatives to traditional offsetting

Organisations wanting to counter-balance their remaining emissions with reductions elsewhere but without confidence in the third-party offsetting firms have two main options:

- Source your own projects
- Use the European Emissions Trading scheme.

Source your own projects

Bigger companies are beginning to research ways of directly offsetting their emissions by investing in projects that they directly control. This would have several benefits. First, the organisation could directly influence the way the offsetting activity operated, providing a further layer of quality control. Second, the company could associate itself much more directly with the project, possibly providing considerable advantages to its public image. Large organisations can already find suitable projects through the specialist offset providers such as Climate Care. Barclays is sponsoring a new generation of efficient cooking stoves in Lesotho. Because Barclays has major interests in southern Africa, this makes excellent sense, not least because its employees in the region can see clearly what the bank is doing.

Use the European Emissions Trading scheme

This option has received very little attention, but may be the most reliable way of ensuring that your organisation's remaining emissions are genuinely balanced by reductions elsewhere.

The European Emissions Trading (ETS) scheme covers about half of the fossil-fuel emissions of major countries including the UK. The biggest emitters, such as power stations and cement companies, are given a fixed yearly allowance of a certain number of tonnes of CO_2. If they actually emit less, they can sell the surplus tonnage. So a company with an allowance of 5 million tonnes but that only needs 4 million tonnes can sell the allowances covering the extra million tonnes. Conversely, a business with a deficiency of carbon allowances needs to cover the deficit by buying more. These allowances are fully tradable and are worth about £19 a tonne at October 2008 prices.

This is what is known as a 'cap and trade' system. The EU has put a cap on total emissions but allows trading between participants. How is this related to offsetting? Each country has a fixed allowance of emissions permits. So if a company not covered by the scheme – and most businesses are far too small to be included – buys allowances in the open market, this action will reduce the total number of permits available to the major greenhouse-gas emitters. Buying 100 tonnes of permits means, at least in theory, that the maximum emissions of major emitters must go down by a similar amount. This purchase has tightened the overall cap. Your 100-tonne purchase will mean that somewhere in the EU a power station or large manufacturing company has been forced to emit less. You have, in effect, offset your own emissions.

I believe that buying emissions permits and then – metaphorically speaking – tearing them up so that no one else can use them is an effective tool for organisations eager to become carbon neutral. Your purchase will very slightly increase the price of permits because the total supply is capped. This price increase will make investment in low-carbon technologies around Europe slightly more attractive for the biggest emitters. So your offsetting activities are directly encouraging the move to a greener economy.

You can buy ETS permits through major banks such as Barclays Capital. For small quantities, it may be cheaper to buy through Ebico, a Witney-based company that sells small lots of permits to individual customers and to small businesses. The price they charge is related to the current cost of the permits on the European carbon exchanges.

What are the disadvantages of this route? First, it is more expensive. An offsetter using projects in Africa might charge £6 or £8 per tonne; the price of ETS permits will be two or three times this. Second, buying 100 tonnes of permits from a broker and claiming you have offset your emissions is not an idea that will be readily understood by your customers or staff. It somehow doesn't feel as effective as paying money to Climate Care to help finance a new wind turbine in China, although it may actually be a more reliable way of reducing CO_2 output. At some level, people may understand that reducing the overall supply of European emissions permits will work as a carbon offset, but it has little emotional appeal.

Ebico is still the only company selling offsets that are based on the withdrawal of permits from the ETS scheme. I wrote to Phil Levermore, the managing director of Ebico, to ask whether he was convinced that his EquiClimate product was a good way of counter-balancing the emissions of a small or medium-sized business. He wrote back saying:

The approach adopted by EquiClimate – withdrawing permits from the market – means that its offsets are robust and reliable and, since the current phase of the ETS covers only the years 2008–2012, offset customers can be reassured that the CO_2 reductions resulting from their decision will take place in the relatively short time-frame we need to tackle climate change.

I think Phil Levermore is right; if we need to offset our remaining emissions, the ETS may offer the best and simplest solution.

'Choice editing'

Imagine you are running a big DIY store. You focus your marketing on green issues and you're proud of your sustainable sourcing of woods and the large range of energy-efficient appliances you stock. But over there in the corner is a selection of propane gas-fuelled patio heaters. Nothing excites the ire of normally mild-mannered environmentalists as much as these wasteful and expensive devices. When in use, they are burning scarce gas to heat the open air and will be consuming more energy than the central-heating system of an entire house in the middle of winter.

Having the display of patio heaters a few yards from the

home-composters or the carefully sourced tropical hardwood garden chairs may affect the image of your store. It undermines the strength of your marketing message – why should customers believe you when you say you are trying to be green? Similarly, it offends those employees who take environmental issues seriously. Journalists who cover your industry are struck by the inconsistency of your approach. A customer buying one of your patio heaters may waste more energy in a week than they save in a year by re-equipping the entire house with low-energy light bulbs.

Increasingly, businesses large and small are allowed to limit the range of products that they sell, taking unacceptable products off the shelves. In fact, consumers will often expect businesses to choose not to sell items that are completely incompatible with the green image that the company is presenting. Although we all generally believe that a company should sell what its customers require, many consumers now want retailers to 'choice edit' what is on the shelves. It may be more profitable not to have the patio heaters on sale if customers are disconcerted when they see them and doubt your claims about your green credentials.

A trusted supplier is allowed to make decisions to no longer stock products that don't meet high green standards and to push products that score highly. Marks & Spencer said to me that its customers expected the chain to work out which goods conform to the business's published climate change and ethical objectives, and no longer stock the articles that fail to meet M&S's strict standards.

Is your business sufficiently trusted by its customers to allow you to focus on the greenest options and stop selling the equivalent to the patio heaters of your industry? If so, you should probably start thinking about pruning the under-performing elements of your product line. And if you don't feel strong enough to do this, should you be worried that your competitors do have the authority to 'choice edit'? Waitrose only sells free-range eggs, but most other supermarkets continue to sell the battery variety. Who is in the stronger position?

Greenwash

The public increasingly believes that most green claims are overstated, or just plain wrong. The reality is that some marketing and advertising material does grossly overstate the degree of benefit that the goods or services provide. Many of the remaining advertisements make claims that don't really stand up when examined closely. Of course, green marketing is no different in this respect to the advertising of conventional goods and services. Nevertheless, unsubstantiated promises are clearly reducing the trust of consumers in brands claiming to be environmentally friendly.

The Advertising Standards Authority (ASA) reports a huge rise in the number of complaints about green claims. The ASA has included rules on green claims as part of its advertising codes (found at www.asa.org.uk/asa/codes/). In 2007, UK consumers protested about the environmental promises in over 400 different advertisements, up nearly five-fold over 2006. Although we shouldn't get too excited about this number – which represents less than 5 per cent of all complaints to the ASA – it shows a heightening level of interest in the quality of green promises made by companies. The ASA says that its research shows that British consumers have high levels of awareness of environmental messages. But in tandem with this, people are also very confused about what these messages actually mean.

This immediately points to the reasons why businesses need to be particularly careful about environmental advertising. It's worth making green statements – customers are interested and will judge your products based on these claims – but they are also very likely to misunderstand what you are saying. And, perhaps equally importantly, your marketing agencies may well be also very unclear about what the advertising actually means. Too many advertisements pushing the green qualities of a product confuse kilowatts and kilowatt hours.

The ASA points to a number of particularly vexing terms that create confusion. The best known is 'carbon neutral'. Some of the most sophisticated and environmentally committed companies in the UK, such as Sky or Barclays, use this expression about their services. But the number of people who actually know what it means is remarkably small. Put at its simplest, it says that a company or single activity generates no net carbon dioxide – any global warming gases produced in creating the goods or service are neutralised by an equal and opposite reduction in greenhouse gases elsewhere. Usually, this means that the company has purchased an 'offset' from another company. These third parties use the money to reduce greenhouse gases somewhere else in the world, perhaps by planting trees, installing small hydro-electric plants or subsidising the installation of energy-efficient cooking stoves in poor countries. Other companies create 'carbon neutrality' by directly investing in renewable energy projects.

Becoming a carbon-neutral business is an extremely worthwhile aim. But any claim that your company has achieved this state should only be made after a rigorous investigation and a check by an independent third party. Your declaration is very likely to be challenged by environmental activists, often with considerable knowledge and considerable scepticism about two things:

- Whether 'offsetting' actually reduces emissions
- Whether the company has accurately calculated the full extent of its emissions.

We've found elsewhere that both of these two questions will often be difficult to answer with complete confidence. If commentators can show that the carbon-neutral claim is implausible, it would generally be better for the company never to have made the claim in the first place.

In fact, all claims about green performance are difficult to robustly support. With pardonable exaggeration, one green marketing guru states that no product can ever be really green. So those soft-focused advertisements on our TV screens about this or that environmentally friendly product are all exaggerating their merits. Making almost everything involves some use of energy and will deplete the earth's resources. This is obviously true in the case of a building made of concrete and steel. But consider the most 'virtual' product you can imagine – perhaps a computer telephony service such as Skype or eBay, the internet auction site. Both of these services need Internet servers and both of them use the worldwide telecommunications infrastructure; they require substantial numbers of people to run and all of these people need to travel and use energy in their offices. Or what about a mobile phone call? You might be surprised to know that someone has actually calculated the carbon cost of using a mobile phone. Over the course of its useful life, the typical phone is responsible for about 100 kg of emissions, which arise from the electricity needed to charge it and to power the base stations. This means that a heavy user might generate over 1 kg a week just from this source. Some forestry may actually be carbon neutral because by encouraging woodlands we are sequestering carbon. Otherwise, almost everything we do in the modern economy adds to the CO_2 in the atmosphere.

So any company that claims that its activities are 'sustainable' is suspect. To be fully sustainable, a company's activities should result in no pollution and no depletion of the world's resources. This is almost impossible. We have unwittingly built a modern economy that encompasses very few truly sustainable activities. This is not to criticise those companies aiming to become exemplars of sustainability, but rather to point out that their task is extremely onerous. Loose claims of sustainability are prime examples of greenwash that make consumers and other businesses extremely sceptical of the real motivations of boastful companies. One business I examined used the word 'sustainability' 28 times in its annual social responsibility report. This company operates coal-fired power stations, one of the the most unsustainable activities on the planet.

Dealing with green activism

Timbmet

Simon Fineman is the managing director of Timbmet, one of the UK's largest importers of tropical hardwoods (www.timbmet.com). In 2005 he provided evidence to a House of Commons committee investigating ways to reduce the importation of illegally logged timber. He opened his remarks by saying:

Probably 12 years ago Timbmet was the leading hardwood importer in the country. We were invaded by Earth First activists who pointed out to us in no uncertain terms that a great deal of the timber we were importing was illegal, and it took us quite a few years after that to come to terms with the fact that as a family-based business we considered ourselves respectable and responsible, and yet we were caught up in what we had to admit was an illegal trade. Despite the fact that we are big relatively, with a turnover of over £100 million and employing 700 people, we felt that we had a responsibility to grab hold of the issue and move it forward; and that is what we have been doing ever since.

Timbmet rose to the challenge from green activists to become perhaps the UK's most responsible timber importer. It is at the centre of efforts to increase the percentage of timber that is sourced both legally and sustainably. As Simon Fineman points out, these two attributes are not the same. Some wood is logged in full compliance with the legal requirements of the source country, but this timber is still not sustainably farmed. Large acreages of valuable forest are still being lost, and Timbmet is in the vanguard of those companies trying to improve the management of the world's forests.

More recently, Simon said:

Governments, legislators, forestry companies, local actors and consumers of forest products and services all need to work together to ensure the long-term integrity of tropical forests, which deliver such a wide range of values to society, both locally and globally.

The 1992 invasion of the Timbmet yard was entirely peaceful. None of the 300 protesters was arrested and no damage caused. The sit-in lasted a few hours and ended in a peculiarly British compromise when the protesters agreed to go home if the workforce left as well and was paid for the day's work. Nevertheless, it exposed the company to scrutiny that it did not welcome, which changed its attitude towards environmental issues. Timbmet is a good example of the increasing number of companies that are now more 'green' than their customers. It devotes considerable effort to working with buyers to educate them on the importance of sustainable sourcing of timber and why it makes sense to buy wood that it is certified by bodies such as the Forest Stewardship Council (FSC).

Simon Fineman points to the core problem. Although many of his customers want their wood to be sustainably sourced, relatively few are prepared to pay for it. He tells the story of one Welsh home-builder asking about sustainable timber for a new development of holiday homes. The conversation was abruptly terminated when the extra cost of £400 a home was mentioned. Few of the construction company's customers would be prepared to pay more for their houses and, quite reasonably, the builder was not prepared to reduce its own margin.

Nor can he source the full range of timber entirely from sustainable sources. Many types and sizes of wood are simply not available. If his business is to serve its customers, he cannot solely stock certified timber – he would soon go out of business. But he can gradually lead his customers towards only specifying sustainable timber in construction and other applications. Separately, Timbmet has set up its own scheme for encouraging wood suppliers to gradually move towards better standards. But every day Simon Fineman faces competitive pressure from companies that are less ethically driven and who are prepared to sell wood that may have been illegally logged. Until customers are better educated and decide that they are prepared to pay the correct price for sustainably sourced wood, Timbmet can only make slow progress to improve standards in this environmentally vital industry.

Innocent Drinks

Innocent Smoothies is one of the greenest businesses in the UK (www.innocentdrinks.co.uk). Its focus on the ethical sourcing of fruit from around the world makes it one of the few businesses to be hugely commercially successful while pursuing an unflinching policy of ensuring its suppliers are paid properly and promptly. Frequently named as one of the best places to work in the UK, Innocent is rightly proud of its extraordinary reputation as a business that takes all green issues very seriously indeed.

Any company in the food industry has to be concerned about the impact of packaging use on the environment. Innocent's statement of principles says:

We aim for four main sustainability characteristics in our packaging:

1   *To use 100 per cent recycled or 100 per cent renewable material in our packaging*
2   *To use the least possible amount of material per pack*
3   *To use materials with a low carbon footprint*
4   *To use materials for which there is a widely available sustainable waste management option.*

In 2007, Innocent accidentally breached these rules. It started selling one of its fruit smoothies in a plastic bottle made from a substance known as PLA (polylactic acid). PLA is made from maize and is marketed by its US manufacturer as a light replacement for oil-based plastics. It is said to be recyclable and compostable, so it appeared to meet the first three of the company's principles. Innocent got one of the relatives of its employees to test whether a smoothie bottle made from PLA would break down in a garden compost heap. He reported success in composting the containers and Innocent started making bold claims for the greenness of this new form of packaging.

Unfortunately, in most circumstances PLA won't break down in domestic compost. Few compost bins maintain a high enough temperature for the long period of time necessary to break down this bio-plastic. If, instead of being composted, the PLA bottle was placed in the plastics recycling bin in the home, it would inevitably be mixed with other conventional plastics such as PET and polypropylene. The addition of PLA bottles to those collected by UK councils wouldn't be a happy outcome because PLA is almost indistinguishable from PET in appearance and cannot be easily separated. The bio-plastic would contaminate the PET waste and make it less valuable to recycling processors. Innocent's use of PLA actually impeded the wider recycling effort rather than helped it.

In addition, Innocent did not appear to realise that PLA is made from genetically modified (GM) maize. Whatever the arguments for and against GM crops, many of Innocent's customers would be uncomfortable drinking a fruit smoothie that had been bottled in a container made from genetically modified maize. Although Innocent had the best of intentions in its eagerness to improve the environmental characteristics of its products, it unwittingly used a product that was neither recyclable nor acceptable to many people in its customer base.

When it identified the problems arising from the non-compostability of PLA in domestic gardens, Innocent immediately removed the bottles from sale. The company replaced them with PET containers made from 100 per cent recycled plastic. This is a much more environmentally friendly alternative and made the company one of the first businesses in the UK to commit to sourcing recycled plastics for all its bottles. Innocent's commitment has had the added advantage of improving the finances of those businesses trying (with difficulty) to establish an effective recycling loop in the UK for PET. In the past, recycled PET for use in the British market has largely come from other countries in northern Europe as waste processors in the UK did not consider it worthwhile separating PET from the stream of plastics waste collected by councils.

The key lesson for Innocent from the aborted attempt to use bio-plastic is the need to carefully investigate the full environmental character of a promising innovation. PLA may have its place as a substitute for oil-based plastics in some applications, but the claims made by its backers exaggerated its suitability for the UK market. In its eagerness to innovate, Innocent was too easily swayed by the sales pitch of its suppliers and did not properly research the true green credentials of a product. A good business loudly (and correctly) proclaiming its solid commitment to environmental and ethical good works will be particularly closely scrutinised. Brand damage from failed innovations like the PLA bottle can be limited by rapid withdrawal of the product and an admission that the experiment had not worked.

A final observation

This book has tried to show that becoming a green company can at times be difficult. However, the rewards will be much more extensive than reduced energy costs and lower carbon emissions. A green company will have more loyalty from employees, a stronger relationship with customers and greater resilience when facing economic shocks. It may not make sense to invest in rising to the top of the 'green ladder' described in chapter 2, but becoming a more environmentally friendly organisation is almost certainly the responsible thing to do, ethically *and* financially.

Appendix

Enhanced Capital Allowances (ECAs)

Businesses can claim 100 per cent first-year capital allowances for equipment that improves energy efficiency or fuel use. This provides an advantage to cash flows in profitable businesses. When a business buys an asset, it can generally only set 20 per cent of the written-down value against its business profits in the year of purchase. Enhanced Capital Allowances raise this figure to 100 per cent. (Loss-making firms can go through a more complex scheme to obtain some financial benefit from buying eligible assets.)

Businesses can claim for capital expenditure in the following categories:

- Energy-saving equipment
- Very low-emission cars
- Water saving.

Energy-saving equipment

This can be in one of 14 different categories:

- Air-to-air energy recovery
- Automatic monitoring and targeting (AMT)
- Boiler equipment

- Combined heat and power (CHP)
- Compact heat exchangers
- Compressed air equipment
- Heat pumps for space heating
- Heating, ventilation and air-conditioning zone controls
- Lighting
- Motors and drives
- Pipework insulation
- Refrigeration equipment
- Solar thermal systems
- Warm air and radiant heaters.

The list of eligible technologies is revised annually. The Carbon Trust keeps a list of qualifying products within each category and only the purchase of new items and necessary installation costs is eligible. Enhanced capital allowances will sometimes only apply to part of the cost of new equipment if not all the expenditure is spent on eligible energy-saving equipment.

New products can be added to the list after applications by manufacturers. The scheme is intended to encourage the purchase of expensive items that may take several years to provide financial payback. Simple energy-saving measures that already make sense financially – such as better insulation – are not covered.

Very low-emission cars

The capital allowances scheme for company cars both encourages the purchase of highly fuel-efficient cars and slightly discourages the use of prestige executive vehicles. Full 100 per cent allowances are available on cars producing less than 110 grammes of CO_2 per kilometre travelled. This is an extremely demanding target, and very few cars currently available in the UK have levels of CO_2 output as low as this. Some example include:

- Toyota Prius (105 grammes per kilometre)
- VW Polo Blue Motion (99 grammes per kilometre)
- Citroën C1 (109 grammes per kilometre)

All electric cars, such as the THINK City or the G-Wiz, are also included.

Cars from 110 to 160 g/km attract a 20 per cent capital allowance for the first year. Most prestige executive cars have higher emissions than this and less fuel-efficient vehicles have a 10 per cent capital allowance per year, making the cash-flow implications of buying these types of car slightly worse than the purchase of other capital assets.

Water saving

Water saving equipment is also covered. A business can claim 100 per cent capital allowances on minor appliances such as showers for employees, and also on large pieces of equipment such as vehicle cleaning machines. Any device that significantly reduces water use is likely to be covered by the scheme.

As with the other technologies, full details are available on the Enhanced Capital Allowances website at www.eca.gov.uk.

The Carbon Reduction Commitment (CRC)

The CRC is a new scheme intended to put a cap on green-house-gas emissions from big electricity users not already covered by the European Emissions Trading Scheme (ETS). The ETS targets intensive users of fuels, such as the power stations, cement plants and steelworks. The CRC is aimed at the next tier of users of electricity and other fuels.

As at the time of writing, the full details of this scheme have yet to be worked out. Nevertheless, organisations that are likely to be covered will be asked to record their total electricity consumption during 2008. To be absolutely clear, eligibility for the scheme is based on electricity use, but the financial effects depend on total energy use and the consequent carbon emissions from this consumption.

An organisation is likely to be included in the scheme if:

- It has at least one site at which electricity is bought through a 'half-hourly' meter and
- Its total electricity consumption is more than 6,000 megawatt hours.

(Please note: increasing numbers of organisations are opting for voluntary half-hour metering. Despite what is sometimes said in the press, it is not the fact that a business has a half-hour meter that matters; the crucial issue is whether the total electricity consumption exceeds 6,000 megawatt hours.)

The electricity use of an organisation is calculated across all its sites and all subsidiaries. This will throw up some anomalies. For example, almost all state schools will be included because they will be grouped under their local authority. But all but the biggest private schools will be exempt because their individual electricity usage will be less than 6,000 megawatt hours. It is not yet clear whether healthcare institutions are covered, but if they are a small private hospital will be outside the scheme but NHS hospitals will be included because the Trust that controls them will, in total, use enough electricity to warrant inclusion.

The UK government has written to about 10,000 organisations to say that they might be included in the scheme. Most people think that about 6,000 businesses, local authorities, other public bodies and NGOs will actually be affected. Broadly speaking, any organisation employing more than about 1,000 employees in an office-based set-up is likely to be caught in the CRC net. However, deciding who is actually responsible for participation in the scheme is a complicated issue. The Defra document describing who is covered by the CRC is 208 pages long and looks at issues such as who is responsible in organisations running PFI/PPP-owned buildings, or whether unincorporated partnerships – such as firms of solicitors operating from several sites – are included. Implementation will not be easy, and we can expect some confusion as the scheme comes into being.

The CRC is intended eventually to resemble a 'cap and trade' system (like the ETS). But it won't start that way. From 2009 until 2012, each participant will pay a fee for each tonne of CO_2 emitted as a result of energy consumption in the organisation. At the moment it seems likely that this figure will be £12 a tonne, which equates very approximately to half a pence per kilowatt hour of electricity use. This is somewhat lower than the current price of allowances under the wider European cap and trade scheme. The low figure is justified by the government on the basis that the price of most electricity bought by medium-sized companies already includes the cost of the European emissions permits, and they are trying to avoid too much double charging.

The important point to understand is that this fee will not be a tax, at least in its early years. All the monies raised in the scheme will be recycled to organisations that have managed to reduce their energy consumption over the previous year. So a business that managed to cut its emissions by 10 per cent in one year might end up as a net beneficiary from the scheme. However, this portion of the scheme will end in 2012.

From 2013, the intention is that the CRC will operate as a fully auctioned cap and trade scheme. Central government will determine a cap for the total emissions from the organisations participating in the scheme, which will be reduced annually. Companies will be able to buy CRC certificates in the auction or, alternatively, buy an equivalent volume in the ETS. This last feature is important: it means that the price of allowances in the CRC can never rise above the price paid in the larger Europe-wide ETS. If it did, the participants would simply switch to buying the cheaper allowances. The intention is to ensure that smaller users can never be put at a disadvantage against the biggest energy consumers.

The Carbon Trust reports that the intention is to use the

scheme to reduce CO_2 emissions by about 4 million tonnes, or slightly under 1 per cent of UK emissions. The Trust also says that business and public sectors excluding those industries covered by the ETS are responsible for about one-third of total UK emissions, so the CRC is probably not going to provide a particularly tight noose to business energy use.

The governmental organisations backing the scheme are confident that it will work well and act as a spur to energy efficiency in organisations that have not traditionally worried too much about carbon emissions. They may be right, but independent observers have a large number of concerns:

- The scheme is proving difficult for participating organisations to understand. Public seminars aimed at bodies involved in the CRC have shown substantial misunderstandings and uncertainties. Of course, this is inevitable at this point. However, a large percentage of organisations attending the seminars report that they are less confident that the scheme is workable on leaving the seminar than when they arrived.

- The large organisations, such as the power generators, participating in the ETS are given their yearly allowances, rather than having to buy them at auction. Why small organisations should pay more than a power station is somewhat unclear.

- Organisations whose operations are covered by Climate Change Agreements (CCAs) are exempt from all or part of the CRC scheme. Climate Change Agreements are deals between industries and government under which the industry agrees to reduce emissions by an agreed percentage in order to escape the Climate Change Levy on energy costs. The interaction between CCAs, the Levy and the new CRC is a complicated and messy area. It can only add to the difficulties of implementing the new CRC.

- The incentives to improve energy efficiency created by the scheme are not great – £12 a tonne for the early years is not a substantial amount of money to save. If we assume that the price at the 2013 auction is the same, then the cost of buying the allowances to cover the typical employee's electricity use will be about £25, or perhaps even less. Yes, it is worth having, but it is not even going to cover the costs of the staff Christmas party.

In the face of these doubts, the sponsoring organisations, principally Defra and the Carbon Trust, have responded by emphasising the value of the scheme in raising the profile of energy saving within an organisation. Particularly stressing the league tables in the first phase of the CRC scheme, they point to the value of success in the scheme to improving the image of the company in the eyes of its stakeholders.

Index